RAJARSI JANAKANANDA
(JAMES J. LYNN)

American self-made business magnate
who became an illumined yogi

Rajarsi Janakananda

(James J. Lynn)

A Great Western Yogi

The Life of Paramahansa Yogananda's
First Spiritual Successor

Self-Realization Fellowship
FOUNDED 1920
Paramahansa Yogananda

Authorized by the International Publications Council of
SELF-REALIZATION FELLOWSHIP
3880 San Rafael Avenue • Los Angeles, California 90065-3298

The Self-Realization Fellowship name and emblem (shown above) appear on all SRF books, recordings, and other publications, assuring the reader that a work originates with the society established by Paramahansa Yogananda and faithfully conveys his teachings.

ISBN 0-87612-019-2
Printed in the United States of America
on recycled paper ♻
10462-8765

CONTENTS

The Spiritual Legacy of Paramahansa Yogananda

A century after the birth of Paramahansa Yogananda, he has come to be recognized as one of the preeminent spiritual figures of our time; and the influence of his life and work continues to grow. Many of the religious and philosophical concepts and methods he introduced decades ago are now finding expression in education, psychology, business, medicine, and other spheres of endeavor—contributing in far-reaching ways to a more integrated, humane, and spiritual vision of human life.

The fact that Paramahansa Yogananda's teachings are being interpreted and creatively applied in many different fields, as well as by exponents of diverse philosophical and metaphysical movements, points not only to the great practical utility of what he taught. It also makes clear the need for some means of ensuring that the spiritual legacy he left not be diluted, fragmented, or distorted with the passing of time.

With the increasing variety of sources of information about Paramahansa Yogananda, readers sometimes inquire how they can be certain that a publication accurately presents his life and teachings. In response to these inquiries, we would like to explain that Sri Yogananda founded Self-Realization Fellowship to disseminate his teachings and to preserve their purity and integrity for future generations. He personally chose and trained those close disciples who head the Self-Realization Fellowship Publications Council, and gave them specific guidelines for the preparation and publishing of his lectures, writings, and *Self-Realization Lessons.* The members of the SRF Publications Council honor these guidelines as a sacred trust, in order that the universal message of this beloved world teacher may live on in its original power and authenticity.

The Self-Realization Fellowship name and the SRF emblem (shown above) were originated by Sri Yogananda to identify the organization he founded to carry on his worldwide spiritual and humanitarian work. These appear on all Self-Realization Fellowship books, audio and video recordings, films, and other publications, assuring the reader that a work originates with the organization founded by Paramahansa Yogananda and faithfully conveys his teachings as he himself intended they be given.

SELF-REALIZATION FELLOWSHIP

Rajarsi Janakananda:
A Great Western Yogi

RAJARSI JANAKANANDA

(JAMES JESSE LYNN)

May 5, 1892–February 20, 1955

Revered president, 1952–1955, of Self-Realization Fellowship and Yogoda Satsanga Society of India.

Ideal disciple of Paramahansa Yogananda for more than twenty-three years.

Rajarsi Janakananda
(James J. Lynn)

"...one of the most sensational American success stories."
—Kansas City Star

"...one of Kansas City's most remarkable stories of individual brilliance and achievement."
—Kansas City Times

"The scope of his activities implies that he is one of the busiest executives in this part of the United States."
—Kansas City Star

"...people who like the ring of the term 'business empire' could put him in the empire class...."
—Kansas City Star

"...I have never seen him when he was not inwardly communing with God."

"...he has attained in samadhi the grace of unshakable peace."

"Because God is reflected in his countenance, his very face sends me into the inner spiritual ecstasy of God's presence."

"In him and in a number of other Occidentals I happily see a fulfillment of Babaji's prophecy that the West, too, would produce saints of true Self-realization through the ancient yogic path."
—Paramahansa Yogananda

One of the most extraordinary and inspiring stories in the annals of modern spirituality lies behind the fact that all of the above statements refer to the same man.

Known to the business world as James J. Lynn, he is revered by countless Self-Realization Fellowship members and friends as Rajarsi Janakananda, beloved and exalted disciple of Paramahansa Yogananda and his first spiritual successor as president of Self-Realization Fellowship/Yogoda Satsanga Society of India.

James Jesse Lynn was born on May 5, 1892, near the small village of Archibald, Louisiana. The remarkable story of his rise from poverty-stricken beginnings to become a self-made millionaire—and of his transformation from business magnate to God-illumined saint—is recounted in the following biographical sketches.

Rajarsi Janakananda outside the Self-Realization Fellowship Hermitage,
Encinitas, California, 1951

James J. Lynn:
An American Success Story

BY DICK FOWLER

Reporter, Kansas City Star, *Kansas City, Missouri*

The following biography, reprinted by permission of the Kansas City Star, *Kansas City, Missouri, was published in that newspaper on May 13, 1951. The article was later included in "Leaders In Our Town," a book by Mr. Fowler on the lives of prominent Kansas Citians.*

At nine o'clock on the morning of the ninth day of the ninth month in the year 1909 a homesick seventeen-year-old youth named Jimmy Lynn got off the train at the old Union Depot. Perhaps even then the something different in his nature was coming to the surface, something that caused him to notice the coincidence of the number 9.

Although the day was Sunday, he walked across the railroad tracks to the Missouri Pacific office above the freight house. Men were working, so he went to work.

Some twelve years later the whole business community of Kansas City knew James J. Lynn, successor to U. S. Epperson, and owner (with a huge debt) of the insurance underwriting company for a large share of the lumber industry. He stood out as a youthful prodigy.

Builder of a "Business Empire"

This year, 1951, people who like the ring of the term "business empire" could put Mr. Lynn in the empire class, at least by Kansas City standards. It spreads into three separate insurance operations, and into oil production, citrus fruits, railroading, and a substantial banking interest. Financially the original Epperson enterprise is now overshadowed by oil, but it is the largest reciprocal fire exchange in the world.

This man who pushes ahead, building and expanding in the world of big business, is unique. In one sense he suggests a mystic in Babylon, a man more concerned with a religious philosophy than with any of the showy or luxurious things that money can buy.

Life Close to Nature

His private office in the R. A. Long Building breathes financial stability: a massive walnut office hung with heavy draperies in the manner of past decades. The bald man behind the heavy desk is bronzed from persistent living outdoors. Life close to nature is part of his creed. His face is so sensitive that you hardly notice the square jaw. There is nothing about him to suggest the bulldog type....

The scope of his activities implies that he is one of the busiest executives in this part of the United States. From this intensely practical life he takes time out for meditation; contemplates the meanings of humanity in the vast scheme of things. Out of these meditations and years of Bible reading and reading from other religions he has developed his own approach to the Christian philosophy. He discusses it freely, but not in a way that is easy for a visitor to understand. Superficially you can say it is wrapped up with the physical and mental side of daily living close to nature. To this writer it suggests a return to the simplicity of Christianity in earlier times when people worshipped in the forests.

The exercises which he takes outdoors (breathing, tensing, and relaxing exercises) may have been suggested by his reading of Oriental religions. This line of study started with a book by E. Stanley Jones, the famous missionary in Asia.*

An Estate of Forest and Orchards and Vineyards

Most Kansas Citians have driven past the 100-acre Lynn estate which lies between Sixty-third Street, Meyer Boulevard, and Paseo and Prospect. For years people have mentioned it in connection with his nine-hole golf course. The golf course was abandoned some years ago.

Beyond the fences and the shelter of dense foliage lie a forest and orchards and vineyards. This is James J. Lynn's outdoor retreat from early spring to late fall. He stays close to the orchards from the early flowering time to the season of harvest, and glows over the opportunity to give away fruits. In the forest are some 2,000 fine hardwood trees

---

* One of the first books on Indian philosophy read by Mr. Lynn was a volume by Mr. Jones, but Mr. Lynn said that he was introduced to Hindu thought through an English translation of the Bhagavad Gita. *(Publisher's Note)*

Mr. Lynn at the site of one of his oil wells, Archer City, Texas, 1950. The J. J. Lynn Oil Division was then in charge of about 25,000 acres of leases in Illinois, Oklahoma, Kansas, and Texas.

which antedate the encroachment of Kansas City. Winters he spends all possible time in southern California where he can continue to live outdoors.

This is the type of life Mr. Lynn manages to find in the midst of the business hurly-burly. While he is nominally vacationing in California he dashes back and forth to business meetings and the large conventions of lumbermen and automobile dealers, the men of the fields where he operates with insurance.

World's Largest Reciprocal Fire Insurance Exchange

His business for the lumber industry has multiplied itself many times to hold the rank of largest reciprocal fire exchange in any industry in the world. His somewhat similar type of reciprocal insurance for American motorcar dealers is not far behind; and within the last eighteen months he has launched a new stock company with full coverage for motorcar owners. It approached the million-dollar mark its first year and appears to be going far beyond that in 1951.

This man absorbed with things of the spirit is a very active oil man. His operations spread over some 25,000 acres of leases in Illinois, Kansas, Oklahoma, and Texas. Financially oil is the biggest of his enterprises, with a gross income from wells that now averages around two million dollars a year.

In the Rio Grande valley of Texas he is a large grower of citrus fruits, with 500 acres in grapefruit and orange groves. As the result of a freeze last January there will be no fruit from the area for two years. But in good times the income from 500 acres has run as high as a half-million dollars in a year.

A railroad job brought him to Kansas City and he is a railroad man today, one of the small group of mid-Westerners who moved to gain control of the Kansas City Southern and the Louisiana and Arkansas railroads from Eastern interests and to lodge the headquarters firmly in Kansas City.

He is a banker: a very large stockholder and the chairman of the executive committee of the Union National Bank.

And this is the man spiritually akin to ancient prophets. Men of a slant only a shade different from his came out of the desert to denounce the splendor and wealth of Babylon.

James J. Lynn at fourteen (*left*) and at seventeen. At fourteen he left home to make his own way in the world. He got an education, while holding full-time auditing positions, by attending evening classes in high-school subjects, accounting, and law. He passed the bar examinations at 21, and at 24 was a C.P.A. James Jackson of the *Kansas City Star* writes: "Mathematicswise, Lynn's IQ would have rung the bell for genius."

One of the "Success Stories, Yet Different From Most"

The business rise of Jimmy Lynn is one of the most sensational American success stories, yet different from most. From the beginning, his talents have been carried by a peculiarly sensitive human being, one who could never bear the thought of any man's ill will.

He was born in 1892 near the crossroads village called Archibald, Louisiana. That long after the Civil War and the reconstruction period, the catastrophe still gripped the family.

Until Jimmy was six, his father was a tenant farmer. Jesse W. Lynn, a neat man with a blond mustache, worked hard to make up for all that had been lost. In the war the family had lost all its lands and slaves. Grandfather Lynn had died from a wound received in the Confederate army. Jesse Lynn had never been given the chance even for normal education.

Eventually the family came into possession of a 120-acre farm that had been salvaged by Jimmy's mother's family, the Archibalds. And that farm was held under a debt to the other heirs.

Jimmy, the fourth of six children, took his turn chopping and picking cotton, but he was the member of the family assigned to help his mother whenever she needed him. She was a dark-eyed little woman, packed with energy; Scotch Presbyterian and saving. Most of Mr. Lynn's memories of his parents are of the hours working by their sides. There was seldom time for relaxation. He still gets pecans from the trees he and his mother set out on the farm.

His first reputation as a prodigy came at the age of five. That was the year he went to the little log schoolhouse two miles away. He was too young to receive much attention from the teacher, so he memorized everything in the Blue Back Speller.

One of the storekeepers at Archibald stood him on a cracker barrel to spell and give definitions, to the amazement of the loafers. Anything in the book—big words like "incompatibility" and "incomprehensible"—he spelled and rattled off the definitions of.

"Well, I swan!" and "I'll be a salted dog!" said the wise men of the corner-store crowd. [When he was a little older] he sat on the porch of this same store, selling fruit from the farm. Butter, he delivered to regular customers who had no cows of their own.

FATHER AND MOTHER OF JAMES J. LYNN

Jesse Williams Lynn, Scottish-Irish, was a farmer all his life. He was proud of his son James, who, when success came, bought for his parents a modern-type home in Archibald, Louisiana. Jesse Lynn died in 1945 at the age of ninety-two. Part of his obituary in the *Beacon-News,* Rayville, Louisiana, read: "His personality was one of rare sweetness and charm. His private life and his associations with neighbors and friends were models of manly virtue and of true and upright citizenship. In him were love of purity; a spirit of tenderness and kindness; Christian integrity and loyalty; loving fidelity to family and friends; delicacy of thought and feeling; a high conception of one's work as the expression of one's character, and, therefore, a holy thing; courage to fight, even to the end, the ills of life; and a soul aglow with Southern warmth."

Salethia Jane Archibald Lynn, of Scottish blood, was born in 1855 into the family after which the town of Archibald (James' birthplace) was named. She died in 1943 at the age of eighty-eight. Extracts from her obituary in the *Beacon-News* are as follows: "She practiced her [Presbyterian] religion and consecrated her life to the welfare of others. She gave her utmost in devoted service, prompted by a heart as open as the gates of day. She shed kindness as the sun sheds light."

A Good Ball Player

His timidity and horror of causing displeasure may have helped his school record. He was shunted around from school to school, to whatever district could afford a teacher that year. And in each, the teacher pointed out Jimmy as an example of top classwork and perfect deportment. He saved himself from the label of "teacher's pet" in baseball. The first game in which the Archibald boys were outfitted in regular baseball suits, they beat the older Mangham town school-team 10 to 2. Jimmy scored four of the runs.

"On His Own" at the Age of Fourteen

The years Jimmy Lynn worked for the Missouri Pacific Railroad were unusual for one thing: when jobs were hard to get there was always a station agent who wanted him. He started at the Archibald station in school time, sweeping out and keeping the freight house in order for $2 a month. At fourteen and graduated from grammar school, he had a job at the Mangham railroad station and made his board and room doing chores at his cousin's hotel.

His first life ambition was fixed on the glamorous office of division superintendent, a life goal that he never achieved. The most impressive figure he knew was W. C. Morse, the division superintendent. In a private car this stern but warmhearted individual of knitted eyebrows traveled up and down the line. Whenever another station agent asked for Jimmy, Morse grumbled that Jimmy was too young, and always let him go.

That was the way he went to Oak Ridge for a temporary job at $35 a month. From there he moved on to Ferriday, the city and division point, at a remarkable $65 a month. When there was a second opening he got the job for his older brother, who married on the strength of it. Slackening business forced a cutback; Jimmy insisted that he was footloose and the one who should go. A traveling auditor for the road was quick to recommend him to a friend with the M.K.&T. railroad at Moberly, Missouri, and that turned out to be the highroad to Kansas City.

Homesickness can be a terrible thing for anyone. More than most teenagers, Jimmy Lynn depended on the warmth and good feeling of human relations. At Moberly he was lost in a world of old people—old men at the office and two old women who rented him a room. One

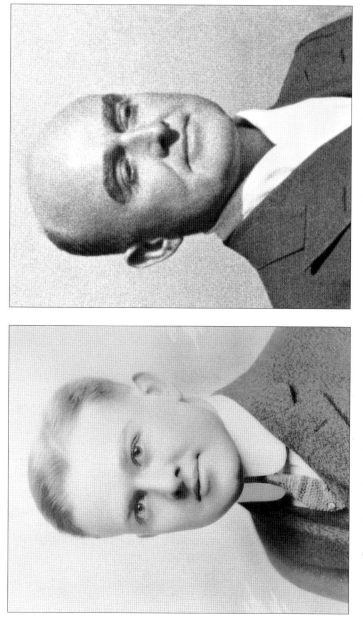

James Lynn at age of twenty-one

Mr. Lynn in 1937

of these women struggled with music lessons and hammered away on the piano until all hours of the night. Then she resented Jimmy's alarm clock that went off early in the morning.

And so he found the job in Kansas City, working for the chief clerk to the Missouri Pacific division engineer. This chief clerk was a man he had known back in Louisiana. From that Sunday of his arrival in Kansas City he felt that he was among friends. Within a little more than seven years he was to be the general manager of the big underwriting company, second only to U. S. Epperson himself.

Promotions came fast. He was employed on the Missouri Pacific in Kansas City as an assistant auditor. In less than a month the auditor was transferred, and a frightened seventeen-year-old Jimmy Lynn handled the auditor's job. He learned it by doing the work and after that he was not afraid of new jobs.

Law School, High School—and a Full-Time Job

But the main theme of the seven years was education. He started from a public school education that had been cut off in the middle of the ninth grade.

About a year and a half after he had come to Kansas City a young assistant planted the idea of getting a legal education at the Kansas City school of law.

The law school exacted Jimmy Lynn's promise to make up the high-school education that he had missed. He carried his full law-school course and high-school subjects at the same time. Within a year he added a correspondence course in accounting to the load—sopped up education in three different fields by night and held a full-time job by day.

At twenty-one, before he had completed his law course, he was admitted to the bar. By that time he had stepped up to become an assistant in the firm of Smith & Brodie, certified public accountants.

Without such items as getting a high-school education and going through law school, Jimmy Lynn's accounting education alone would have been a prodigious undertaking. Two local accountants offered night courses to the correspondence school students, and Jimmy took them. On his own, he read everything in accounting he could find and worked out all the problems.

(LEFT) Mr. Lynn at the age of twenty-nine, when he became the owner of U. S. Epperson Underwriting Co. (RIGHT) Mr. Lynn in his Kansas City office, about 1937. "If we are at peace within our beings, we can harmoniously carry on our duties even in the business sphere," Mr. Lynn said. "We can accomplish admirable things in the world without necessarily clashing with others. Eventually we can perform all our duties with the full consciousness of God's presence."

Mr. Lynn sampling one of the grapefruits from his 500-acre orchard in the Rio Grande Valley of Texas, 1947. Of him Paramahansa Yogananda said: "His whole existence is an exalted one, even though he attends to heavy business duties and is required to travel extensively in connection with his business responsibilities. He has had many temptations thrown in his way, but he has not succumbed to them. He has felt that Joy within which is greater than anything the world can offer. 'Lord, Thou art more tempting than any other temptation.'"

Passed C.P.A. Examination; Highest Grade on Record

Under the rules of the state board, nobody could become a certified public accountant before the age of twenty-five. Long before that age Jimmy Lynn was handling involved, top-bracket accounting jobs for Smith & Brodie. When he was twenty-four he passed the state examination with the highest grade on record to that time. Confronted with such evidence, the board waived the age rule and gave him his C.P.A. certificate at twenty-four. By that time he had a twenty percent interest in the [accounting] firm.

It was during this period of high-pressure education that Jimmy Lynn met and courted Miss Freda Josephine Prill of Kansas City. They were married in October 1913.

Along with the urge to please everybody, Jimmy Lynn seems to have been born with unusual curiosity. It was his nature to look for the explanations of everything. For a curious individual, accounting can be an exciting adventure. Figures tell the story of a business, how it operates, and what makes it tick.

In Kansas City young Lynn was assigned to accounting work for the U. S. Epperson Underwriting Company and the Lumberman's Alliance which it serves. In Chicago and St. Louis he audited other reciprocal insurance exchanges. The figures were business education....

Lynn Investigated With a Typical Thoroughness

Circumstances brought together the boyish Jimmy Lynn and the weighty Epperson. Lynn was assigned to audit the affairs of a burned-out Mississippi mill which happened to be a case that had particularly concerned U. S. Epperson. On the way to Mississippi, Lynn read Epperson's voluminous file and made a point of answering all the questions that had been raised. His audit revealed a clear motive for arson. Epperson showed that he was impressed. It happened at a critical time.

Death took H. A. Thomsen, the underwriting company's general manager, and Epperson was like a man who had just lost his right hand. He called on Lynn to straighten out some of his personal affairs, then offered him the job of treasurer in the company. Lynn refused.

Late at night, while he worked over the books in this office, Jimmy Lynn felt Epperson's eyes on him. And from time to time he heard the words, "I wish you weren't so young."

A Westerner in *samadhi* (superconsciousness), January 1937, Encinitas. Mr. Lynn said: "The love and joy of God that I feel is without any end. One can never forget it once he has tasted it; it is so great he could never want anything else to take its place."

Out of that situation came an offer of the top job of general manager. At the age of twenty-four, barely arrived at the status of C.P.A., Jimmy Lynn had the experience of competing powers bidding for him. Epperson started with an offer of $5,000 a year and worked it up to an arrangement that amounted to $12,000. The salary was so precedent-shaking that Lynn was sworn to secrecy, and it has been a secret to this time. Fred A. Smith, head of the accounting firm, countered by offering Lynn a full partnership which was probably worth more than Epperson's $12,000.

It wasn't salary that tipped the scales but opportunity. Epperson spoke of his age and of the chance to take full responsibility within a very few years. The opportunity turned out to be greater than Jimmy Lynn knew, and also far more precarious.

The hope of someday taking over full management for Epperson ended in 1921; Epperson decided to sell. He was ill and fearful that something would occur to destroy the value of his business. He wanted to put his affairs in order.

A frantic Jimmy Lynn proposed that he should buy the business himself. Epperson stated the very obvious fact, "You don't have the money."

A Risky Loan That Produced Great Results

In his later years E. F. Swinney, head of the First National Bank, talked about Jimmy Lynn as his No. 1 example of a risky loan that produced great results. Swinney elaborated with the enthusiasm of a man who might have been criticized or kidded for his daring.

The size of the loan which was the purchase price of the company has never been made public. It stood somewhere high in the hundreds of thousands and it was made strictly on the character of a young man who was not yet thirty years old. The notes were handled through the bank, but it was generally understood that Swinney had personally guaranteed the loan.

When Lynn produced a check for the full amount of the purchase price, U. S. Epperson was so dumbfounded that he took a month to decide to accept the check and sign the contract.

The Epperson Company had originated with a problem in the lumber industry. Because of the fire hazards at lumber mills in early years they were unable to get insurance for more than three fourths their value and that only at exorbitant rates. In 1905 R. A. Long and other leaders of the industry organized the Lumbermen's Underwriting Alliance which was set up to spread the individual's risk throughout many companies in the industry, the group standing ready to make up the fire losses of any one (of the members). U. S. Epperson formed his company to handle the insurance for the Alliance on a flat percentage basis. From the beginning it was a choosy arrangement in which the poor risks were not admitted to the Alliance. Those who took the necessary steps to protect themselves against loss by fire received full insurance at reasonable cost.

In 1917, when Jimmy Lynn became the Epperson general manager, the insurance premiums ran somewhere less than a million dollars a year, and the resources of the Lumbermen's Underwriting Alliance were under a million. Today the annual premiums are around six millions, and the resources have grown to more than thirteen millions.

Rapid Progress Under Lynn

A period of rapid growth started immediately after Lynn bought the Epperson business. He attributed it to the talents of people in the organization. These talents were encouraged by his policy of turning people loose to show what they could do, a policy that also involved paying salaries according to demonstrated ability. As summed up by one employee, it was a case of opening the door to individual opportunity.

The prodigious loan made by E. F. Swinney could have been paid back in three or four years. Such were the profits from the stimulated business. When the loan was reduced to manageable size, Lynn chose to expand. The second year he moved into the field of reciprocal insurance for motorcar dealers. They had formed their own Universal Underwriters exchange which had $57,000 of premiums when Lynn took over the management. The exchange now has premiums of around $4,500,000, and covers one-fourth of the factory-authorized dealers in the country. Like the lumber companies, the automobile dealers come into their exchange on a highly selective basis that holds down the total.

The Lynn sideline in citrus fruits started in 1927 with a twenty-acre ranch. He discovered that he couldn't get top management for a ranch that size, so he expanded to 500 acres.

His oil business started in 1938 on the kind of a deal he wouldn't take today. In the middle of a large Illinois oil field, a stubborn farmer held out for $50,000 as the price of a lease on 100 acres. The big and experienced operators wouldn't take it. Lynn paid the $50,000 and got a dry hole for a start. The second drilling job produced one of the best wells in the field and he was on his way.

A Philanthropic Gesture for a Beloved City

The only strictly public job accepted by James J. Lynn was service on the park board. It might have been connected in his mind with reverence for the outdoors and life close to nature.

After he had resigned from the board he had an opportunity to sell the tract of land on Sixty-third Street for an outdoor theater. It happened to be near the new Sixty-third Street entrance of Swope Park, so Mr. Lynn telephoned J. V. Lewis, the park superintendent. Lewis had been saddened by the thought of a private business beside the new entrance.

"Well, the only way to make sure the park is protected is to put the land in the park," said Mr. Lynn. "I'm giving it to the city."

MR. LYNN'S LAST HOME, BORREGO SPRINGS, CALIFORNIA

Mr. Lynn was born on a farm and died on a farm. His birth took place in a one-room log cabin; his death occurred in a spacious well-appointed home on a 668-acre estate, Lynn Farms, in Borrego Springs, California, on February 20, 1955. He often reflected on life's contrasts: an expression of the inexorable law of relativity that governs the phenomenal world. "God is the only Immutable," he said, "the only Security."

SAINT LYNN (RAJARSI JANAKANANDA), 1933

Paramahansa Yogananda remarked: "As my great Master said years ago, 'You will find some saintly souls in America.' And I really believed it when I saw Mr. Lynn. I hope you will all follow his saintly example."

Saint Lynn: The Business Magnate Who Became God-Illumined

(From "Rajarsi Janakananda: A Centennial Tribute")

Though the extraordinary outer success of James J. Lynn won him the deep respect of the business community, newspaper accounts of his life do not fully reveal his supreme achievement in life—his inner spiritual attainment. So great was his spiritual advancement through Kriya Yoga that Paramahansa Yogananda referred to him as Saint Lynn. The following account, taken from an article published in Self-Realization *magazine in commemoration of Rajarsi's birth centennial in 1992, sheds more light on the spiritual side of this self-made millionaire who became a God-realized master through India's ancient science of yoga.*

It was in January 1932 that James J. Lynn met his guru, Paramahansa Yogananda, who later bestowed on him the spiritual title and name of Rajarsi Janakananda.* By that time, Rajarsi was a financial success by any standard. His inner life, however, was another matter. "My life was business," he later said, "but my soul was sick and my body was decaying and my mind was disturbed. I was so nervous I couldn't sit still."

"I was a totally frustrated man," he recounted on another occasion. "I had thought money could give me happiness, but nothing seemed to satisfy me. I lived in a state of nervousness, a state of strain, an inward state of uncertainty. Then I met Paramahansa Yogananda and started to practice yoga."

That meeting proved to be the most significant turning point in the life of Rajarsi Janakananda. It also marked a new era in the history of

---

* The monastic name Rajarsi Janakananda was bestowed on Mr. Lynn by Paramahansa Yogananda in 1951. (See page 47.) To avoid the confusion of two names, Rajarsi is referred to by his monastic name throughout this article.

Paramahansa Yogananda's world mission.* "Shortly before meeting Rajarsi," Sri Daya Mata has written, "the Guru had passed through grave times trying to keep his work from total collapse. It was a period of great upheaval in the society; and the burdens, financial and otherwise, seemed almost insurmountable. Recognizing Paramahansaji† as his divine guru, and embracing the Self-Realization Fellowship teachings as his everyday way of life, Rajarsi also assumed many of the financial burdens of the society."

The scriptures of India say that when a great master comes to this world with a God-ordained mission for the upliftment of humanity, he brings with him advanced disciples from past incarnations to assist his work. In a talk in 1942, Paramahansaji referred to this, saying: "A great saint in India used to cry, 'O my dear ones, where are you? Wherever you are, come to me.' And one by one they came as his disciples in this life. So it is with these close disciples around me: I knew them before....When I heard the name of Mr. Lynn I knew that I had known him before. I knew that such a one would be sent to me."

In a 1932 letter to ashram residents at Self-Realization Fellowship headquarters in Los Angeles, Paramahansaji wrote: "Lecture campaign work at Kansas City and meeting some of the most spiritual Yogoda students there has been one of the greatest happinesses of my life." Such was Rajarsi's receptivity that in that first meeting, in January 1932, the Guru was able to transmit to him the experience of *samadhi,* ecstatic union with God. In a lecture in 1933, Paramahansaji said: "A wealthy Kansas City man, the first day we met, touched Christ Consciousness. His soul was ripe. When he received the Kriya technique he said, 'Life boils within my spine. That is the technique I have been seeking. I have found God.'‡ He meditated six hours with me the first day."

---

* See pp. 184–85. Paramahansa Yogananda had been sent to America from India by his Guru in 1920, to found Self-Realization Fellowship as the means of disseminating worldwide the ancient spiritual science of Kriya Yoga. (In India Paramahansa Yogananda's work is known as Yogoda Satsanga Society. He also used "Yogoda" to refer to his work in America in the early years.)

†The suffix "ji" is customarily added to names in India as a means of expressing respect.

‡Reference to Kriya Yoga, an advanced technique of meditation taught by Paramahansa Yogananda in the *Self-Realization Fellowship Lessons,* which enables the practitioner to centralize the life energy in the spine and brain, effecting a blissful awakening of the subtle spiritual centers of divine perception.

Paramahansaji and Mr. Lynn, Self-Realization headquarters, January 14, 1933—one year after their first meeting. "Some people say, 'The Western man cannot meditate.' That is not true," Master declared. "Since Mr. Lynn first received *Kriya Yoga*, I have never seen him when he was not inwardly communing with God."

Balancing Business Success and Spiritual Success

Even after his profoundly transforming spiritual awakening, Rajarsi continued a full schedule of business activities for another twenty years. Though he now devoted more time to his spiritual life and less to his corporation, his business continued to grow and prosper. However, the requirements of his business prevented Rajarsi from remaining for long periods in the Guru's ashram; and he was well acquainted with the difficulties of keeping centered in God while living in a demanding worldly environment. He once wrote to Paramahansaji:

> Only my love for Divine Mother is wanted. How distressed I am when pulled away from Her and from communion with Her loved ones. I cannot live *of* the world and would prefer not to live *in* it. Drinking, smoking, and worldliness, selfishness in business and otherwise, just kill my soul—it is this environment that causes me such intense suffering. Will meditate and try to get away from the world. Am with you in spirit....how joyful it would be to be with you in person. But there are yet many things I must do before my work and business are in condition for me to leave again. I am looking forward with deepest earnestness to my return home. What a heavenly blessing that will be. Please do write often....Even short notes or just a word from your heart help to sustain me to a degree that I know it is hard for you to realize. When one knows the sweetness of Heaven on earth and is snatched away by worldly environment he suffers the agonies of hades, but my heart will be stout enough to carry on.

> Divine blessings, devotion, and boundless love,
> Your little boy

That stoutness of heart and his Guru's loving guidance enabled Rajarsi to persevere in his spiritual efforts despite all outer distractions, until he was firmly established in the divine consciousness. Sri Daya Mata, president of Self-Realization Fellowship/Yogoda Satsanga Society of India since 1955, has described how Rajarsi was able to balance his spiritual life with the demands of his business empire: "Master* told him: 'I make one request of you—that in spite of your many responsibilities,

---

*"Master" is a respectful title often used by disciples when referring to Paramahansa Yogananda—one who had attained self-mastery. It serves as an English equivalent for "Guru," the customary Sanskrit term for one's spiritual preceptor.

Guru and disciple, Encinitas, 1938. "How heavenly it is to enjoy the company of a saint!" Rajarsi said. "Of all the things that have come to me in life, I treasure more than all else the blessings Paramahansaji has bestowed on me."

you arrange your schedule so that you have a period of meditation each day.' Rajarsi resolved to follow his Guru's instructions, no matter how difficult it might be. Conditions at his home were not favorable, so he arose early each morning and went to his office to meditate. To insure that he was not interrupted, he would leave a note on his secretary's desk, which she would see when she came to work: 'I am in conference. Please do not disturb.' He smiled when he said to us: 'Of course, I never let on that I was "in conference" with God.' The staff may not have understood what he was doing, but they had tremendous respect for him; and it was accepted that until ten a.m. every day, he was 'in conference.' This continued for all the years from the time he met Master until his retirement. It was the foundation of his liberating spiritual progress."

As Rajarsi deepened in God-realization, Paramahansaji often publicly referred to him as "Saint Lynn." On one occasion the Guru said: "As my great Master said years ago, 'You will find some saintly souls in America.' And I really believed it when I saw Mr. Lynn. I hope you will all follow his saintly example."

The Simplicity of a Great Soul

Though in his outer activities Rajarsi expressed the dynamic will and drive-to-accomplish necessary to create a business empire, to those who knew him as a devotee of God it was his quiet humility that most characterized his personality. "I have never seen anyone more humble than he," Paramahansaji often said. Rajarsi signed most of his letters to his Guru "Little one," or simply with a small dot followed by a one.

Sri Daya Mata has described the humble simplicity of this great soul, which so impressed her when she met Rajarsi in 1933 during his first visit to Mt. Washington (SRF Headquarters in Los Angeles):

"One evening Master called me to his kitchen and asked me to bring him a needle and a spool of black thread. He was holding a pair of suspenders. When I had brought the requested articles he began to sew up a rent in the suspenders. I quickly offered to do the work, but he replied: 'Oh, no, I will fix these myself. Can you imagine! Mr. Lynn has worn these same suspenders for ten years.' Master was filled with delight and affection, realizing that although Mr. Lynn could have purchased almost anything, he had lived so simply that one pair of suspenders had been worn and mended over a period of ten years.

"This incident left an indelible impression on my mind. Truly Rajarsi was one of those great devotees who had learned to live 'in the world, but not of it.' His simplicity was untouched by the material success he had achieved. He was the most humble of men, his mind ever remaining fixed on God."

Brother Bhaktananda, a Self-Realization Fellowship monk since 1939, has said: "Rajarsi Janakananda was a very quiet person. He spoke very little, except perhaps to give us a few suggestions about meditation. On several occasions he asked me to walk with him on the ashram grounds. He kept silent for the most part; but from time to time he would say, almost as if marveling to himself: 'What Master has done for me! What Master has done for me!' He never talked about all the things he had done for Master—only what Master had done for him."

"He hardly talked when he was with us," recalls Brother Ananda-moy, a member of the Self-Realization Fellowship Board of Directors. "When he said anything, it was 'Master's light; Master's love.' He was so absorbed in it; he radiated it."

A Message From Swami Sri Yukteswar

In 1935 Paramahansaji was summoned back to India by his guru, Swami Sri Yukteswar. That great Master knew his time to leave the earth was fast approaching, and recalled his beloved disciple for one last visit. Rajarsi generously provided the funds for Paramahansaji's journey. (Extracts from letters written by Paramahansaji to Rajarsi during the trip are printed on pages 63–133.)

Sri Yukteswarji entered *mahasamadhi* a few months after Paramahansaji and he were reunited. Following are excerpts from a letter written by Paramahansaji to Rajarsi—seven months after Sri Yukteswar's passing:

October 1, 1936

There is just a thin screen of ether between the world and Master [Sri Yukteswar]. He is more real to me than ever, and of great influence, for he is guiding me without the impediments of a body and worldly limitations. Whenever I have arrived at a crossroad in my life he has torn the ether as if with a knife and shown himself unto me. All that he said during his lifetime on earth he is repeating within me now: "Yogananda, I am not only in Serampore but everywhere, and from Omnipresence I shall guide thee." It is wonderful to find that all things he told about are being brought to fruition. He often tells me to say how sorry he is not to have given a written message for you while he was still in the earthly body. He is now writing through me as I write to you:

"Beloved son, your life and actions have glorified us. You are a celestial instrument. Expand fearlessly in the realm of renunciation for the cause of Self-Realization, India, and humanity. India's spiritual habits mark your forehead. Your actions are joyfully recognized and witnessed by the All-Supreme and by the Gurus."

After I had received the above message, Sri Yukteswar vanished from within and I was at once called away on some urgent work; so now I start to write to you after a lapse of two days. My Guru wanted to tell something more to you, but he must have felt somebody was going to call me. Whenever I hear from him about you and me I will tell you. This is very sacred and strange. What is unreal to millions is real to me.

My heart is purged of all desires except the desire for the fulfillment of the duties assigned to me and to you; after that, wherever I am, I shall roam in the ether, blessing you constantly, guiding you with my love and life until I meet you in the Father's mansion. That is my task, and ever I am grateful that by your nobility and constant effort you have made it easy for me to work to that end. That is my inspiration to write to you, for my letters to you are letters that God writes through me. Compare and reread each line of all the letters I write to you and you will feel His presence. I feel the same in most of your letters, for none in this world has so well responded to me and drawn so much love out of me. In purity and blessedness I will deliver you unto the Lord.

Many years, since childhood, I dreamed of somebody that would be pure, exemplary, God-bent alone, and powerful to accomplish in the world. God fulfilled my desire: in you I behold an ideal one who loves me unconditionally. The love of parents, of woman, is imperfect, as they have the compulsion of instinct or sex attraction; but love between souls like you and me is perfect, for there is only pure unconditional surrender. I love you not only because of what you are now, but because you were sent to me that I express toward you a perfect divine love.

When I leave the mortal coil and enter the Omnipresent Electricity—God's great love came over me just now as I thought of your dear self. I'm happy beyond dreams, finding so much happiness in you.

Whenever I am with you I want to talk only of God. I do not like to talk of negative things. This rule I have faithfully observed and would ever like to observe; for I never can brook any breach of unloveliness even to touch your sacredness. My words to you encourage you to race endlessly for more and more perfection. Ever expand in God until you behold the body changed into energy, the mind into the greater mind, and your soul into Spirit.

The Encinitas Hermitage Years

When Paramahansaji returned from India, a special surprise had been prepared for him by Rajarsi—a hermitage overlooking the Pacific Ocean at Encinitas, California. In his *Autobiography of a Yogi,* Paramahansaji wrote:

"During my stay in India and Europe (June 1935 to October 1936), Mr. Lynn had lovingly plotted with my correspondents in California to prevent any word from reaching me about the construction of the ashram in Encinitas. Astonishment, delight!

"During my earlier years in America I had combed the coast of California in quest of a small site for a seaside ashram. Whenever I had found a suitable location some obstacle had invariably arisen to thwart me. Gazing now over the sunny acres in Encinitas, humbly I saw the fulfillment of Sri Yukteswar's long-ago prophecy: 'a retreat by the ocean.' "

As often as he was able to leave his business, Rajarsi would join his Guru at the new retreat. Paramahansaji remarked during this period, "In the Encinitas hermitage, St. Lynn and I have been meditating day and night. I have a hard time even getting him to eat or sleep. In this country I have never before known such unity and friendship, such divine communion."

Durga Mata, a disciple of Paramahansa Yogananda from 1929 until her passing in 1993 (a Board member and Secretary of Self-Realization Fellowship until her retirement in 1986), was assigned by Paramahansaji to look after the cooking, secretarial, and other such needs of Rajarsi when he was in residence in Encinitas—a blessed duty she fulfilled until Rajarsi left his body in 1955. In an informal gathering with devotees, she shared some of her personal recollections: "To see Master and Rajarsi together was one of the sweetest things you could experience; it was like glimpsing a bit of heaven. Master's eyes became liquid pools of divine love, as when a mother looks at her child—only much, much more. Each time they met it was as though they were meeting for the first time—their relationship was always new. That is what pure love is; it never grows old. In Master and Rajarsi we saw the highest expression of the pure love of the guru and disciple relationship—the melting, the blending, of pure love.

"Rajarsi was both very spiritual and very methodical—he wasn't born with material wealth; his success came because he earned it. His

Two views of Self-Realization Fellowship Hermitage—a gift from Rajarsi to Paramahansa Yogananda in 1936—overlooking the Pacific Ocean, Encinitas, California. Elsewhere on the spacious grounds are ashram residences and a Self-Realization Fellowship Retreat. An SRF Temple is nearby.

material environment made many demands on him, but he was very strong-willed and high-principled: he never drank, he never smoked, he never swore, he was always honest. When I first met him he was more business than spiritual—except when he was in Master's presence. Gradually through meditation the balance came between business and spirituality. He did not have it easy. He fought for his meditations, and he won. Towards the end, he was all spiritual, and businessman nil.

"After Master left his body, I would sometimes read to Rajarsi from letters Master had written to him. Rajarsi was not an emotional person at all; but when he felt Master's love, tears would come to his eyes—not tears of sorrow that Master was no longer in the body, but tears of love. As though experiencing for the first time the unconditional love of the Guru for his disciple, he would say, 'I did not know he loved me so much!' He would just become drowned in that love, inwardly dancing in that love. He would repeat over and over: 'Joy, joy, Master's joy! Love, love, Master's love!'"

A Perfect Divine Friendship

Sri Daya Mata has described the perfect divine friendship that existed between these two lovers of God, one the Master, one the disciple—him whom Paramahansaji called his "little one" and his "most blessed beloved little one."

"During those times when Master and Rajarsi were in Encinitas together, every evening at sunset they could be seen walking hand in hand like two small children, up and down the flagstone path on the lawn in front of the Hermitage. Their eyes would be shining with the love and friendship they shared with God and with each other. Sometimes Master would be speaking about some deep philosophical subject, and then his 'little one' would remain quiet, listening intently. At other times both would be silent, absorbed in the inner bliss.

"Never have I seen such a sweet friendship and such a reverential relationship as that expressed between these two divine souls. With hearts lifted on high with inspiration, and with a lump in our throats, we young disciples, along with dear Gyanamata, used to stand by the windows, following with our gaze and devotion these two whose companionship is epitomized in Master's poem, 'Friendship.'* We never felt

---

* In *Songs of the Soul,* published by Self-Realization Fellowship.

shut out—our hearts' devotion became one with theirs as our consciousness merged in a transcendent union at the feet of Divine Mother."

Brother Premamoy, a Self-Realization Fellowship monk who met Rajarsi in 1952, once said: "The friendship between Master and his disciple Rajarsi Janakananda demonstrated perfectly the ideal of respect as the basis of all human relationships. Our Guru treated Rajarsi as a friend, and also as a son, but at the same time as a disciple. And Rajarsi gave Master the same kind of respect—as to a friend, to a father, and above all, to the guru. At times, their relationship was expressed in a childlike simplicity.

"Yet beyond the friend, beyond the father, it was mainly the guru that Rajarsi saw in Paramahansaji. Master often said that Rajarsi had fulfilled one-hundred percent the wishes of his heart. This was not a statement lightly made by our Guru. Rajarsi's attitude of complete re-

Handwritten notes from Rajarsi to Paramahansaji. So humble was this ideal disciple that he frequently signed his notes to the Guru "Little one," or simply with a small dot followed by a one. When staying at Encinitas, Rajarsi supervised the work in the vegetable gardens as his ashram task. These notes accompanied offerings of produce from Rajarsi to his Guru.

Master   3/18

Peas from my pockets and my heart for your breakfast. My love. Pick more for your use while I am away

•1

Master   3/18/47

These avocados are from my pockets and my heart for you. They are tree ripened. Eat heartily of them with my love

•1

spect had enabled him to achieve perfect attunement with the Guru and become a liberated soul."

Rajarsi's relationship with his Guru was characterized by a profound receptivity to every nuance of the Guru's spiritual counsel. Paramahansaji once said: "When students ask me why Saint Lynn was able to make such rapid spiritual progress, I reply: 'He knows how to listen.' "

An Exemplar of the Guru's Teachings

It was because of Rajarsi's perfect mastery of the Self-Realization Fellowship teachings that Paramahansaji so often extolled him publicly as an example for all on the path. Brother Anandamoy has said: "Near the end of Master's life, Guruji asked Rajarsi to say a few words to the assembled guests and disciples at a Christmas banquet. In Master's presence Rajarsi always tried to stay in the background, avoiding the limelight. So he said to Master: 'Oh, no, you talk. You can do it so much better than I.'

"The instant he uttered these words, however, he got up and started to address the gathering. He realized that he had contradicted his Guru; he had shown reluctance when Master had asked him to do something. Immediately he corrected himself. There was not a second of delay.

"He had a very soft voice, and quietly he said, 'I have the Christ Consciousness. Nobody has to tell me what it is. I know. I have experienced it.' Then he said, 'When the ego steps out, God steps in. When the ego steps in, God steps out. There is not room for both.' There was not a trace of pride in his words; it was simply his humble, sincere testimony to what one can attain through practice of these teachings."

Another disciple of Paramahansaji has related an example of the great humility of this exalted soul: "I remember an encounter with Rajarsi at the formal opening of the Lake Shrine. After the dedication ceremony, which was conducted by Master, many of the guests congregated around the grounds in little groups. This went on for quite some time.

"Rajarsi came over by the Gandhi Memorial, and was talking to a group of about eight or ten people. He was discussing the sacred experience of communion with the *Aum,* and the state of Cosmic Consciousness. My mother, who didn't know Rajarsi, was part of that group. And as he was describing Cosmic Consciousness, my rather gregarious

Mr. Lynn in meditation, Encinitas, August 1953. He often said: "On the path of Self-realization one feels the divine Life within him. He experiences the union of his individual soul with universal Spirit."

mother interrupted: 'Well! I can explain that much better.' Imagine!

"I moved over to her as quickly as I could. I kept trying to poke her with my elbow, but she continued her 'discourse.' Then I tried stepping on her foot. At last in desperation I blurted out: 'Mother, you don't know who you're talking to!' And she finally stopped. I then introduced them: 'Saint Lynn, this is my mother. Mother, this is Saint Lynn, and he knows God.'

"He greeted her very graciously; there was absolutely no sign of offense. My mother apologized right away: 'I'm so sorry. I didn't know who you were.' With childlike humility, Rajarsi said: 'Oh, that's all right. One can never know all of God. He is ever new, always expanding. He just goes on and on expanding throughout eternity—ever new Joy.'

"What a beautiful explanation! It made a tremendous impression on me. Here was an active American businessman, not a hermit who was free to meditate in a Himalayan cave. Yet he could apply these teachings to his life and manifest complete realization of their truth. This is a real ray of hope for the rest of us Westerners! He was still busy in the world at that time, looking after his business responsibilities. But his consciousness was at all times totally absorbed in God and Master."

Paramahansaji often pointed out to those who admired Rajarsi's business accomplishments that his spiritual achievements were far more important. "I remember one evening when Master and I were walking on the lawn in front of the Hermitage," recalled Meera Mata, a close disciple of Paramahansaji's. "Rajarsi was sitting on the ground in lotus posture. Without saying anything, Master took me by the hand and led me quietly away. When we had gone some distance, Master said, 'Let us not disturb him. Rajarsi is doing more good by the depth of his meditations than by all the money he has given to the work. If only you could all realize how important meditation is. In changing yourself you have already changed thousands. Always remember Rajarsi sitting here meditating and serving me in this way.' "

In 1951, after the last Kriya Yoga initiation ceremony that Paramahansaji conducted, the Guru bestowed upon his disciple formal vows in the ancient monastic Swami Order. He gave him the name of Rajarsi Janakananda, and announced that he would be his first successor as president of the worldwide society. "He has mastered *sabikalpa samadhi*," Paramahansaji informed those present, "and

A LETTER TO PARAMAHANSA YOGANANDA
IN MR. LYNN'S HANDWRITING

*"I have dived deeper into God than ever before,
and wherever I go will be with Him"*

Encinitas, Calif.
April 22nd [1951]

Blessed Beloved Master:

Just a short last note before my departure for Kansas City. It is difficult to realize that I must depart this holy environment and cast myself again into the busy and noisy environment. I have dived deeper into God this time than ever before, and wherever I go will be with Him.

The dates you sent are delicious and I have eaten generously of them since they came. The variety gives me a change from the Deglet Noors [dates grown in Indio, California] although all are good and the change is welcome and enjoyed. The Deglet Noors are the best—so you and I think. Thank you for your loving thought of me.

Good-bye for a while, and with all my blessings and love,

Little one

he is rapidly approaching the *nirbikalpa* state."*

Spiritual Successor to Paramahansa Yogananda

The *mahasamadhi*† of Paramahansa Yogananda in 1952 was a catastrophic blow to the Guru's thousands of followers worldwide. Many wondered, "How will this work go on without a living guru?" Mrinalini Mata, close disciple of Paramahansaji's and vice president of Self-Realization Fellowship, has observed: "Often, when a spiritual leader leaves the body, his work gradually dies out. But you will see that though Paramahansaji's *mahasamadhi* was so many years ago, his spiritual family, his society, is growing steadfastly. Why? Because those whom Guru chose to represent him in the leadership of his organization have had the humility, and the divine attunement with God's will, to keep before all who come, not themselves, but the image of God alone, Guru alone."

The first Self-Realization Fellowship Convocation after Paramahansaji's passing was held in July 1952. Rajarsi, as the new president of Self-Realization Fellowship, was scheduled to speak. Brother Anandamoy recalls:

"Many members expected that Rajarsi would assume the role of Guru (not knowing that Master had declared that it was God's will that he be the last in the line of SRF Gurus), because they thought they had to have a guru in the body, one whom they could see and hear. It would have been very easy for Rajarsi to have proclaimed himself Guru because of his great spiritual power and magnetism. But what he said at that gathering firmly established the course of Self-Realization Fellowship for all future generations. Very simply, in a quiet voice, he told the members, 'There will be no other guru. Master will always be our guru.'

* Rajarsi recounted how, some months after Paramahansaji's passing, the Master's blessing enabled him to achieve the highest state of *nirbikalpa samadhi*. Brother Anandamoy recalls: "Rajarsi said that for three days, he had a complete spiritual blackout. In his meditations he felt absolutely nothing, no matter how much he tried. And for a person who had mastered *sabikalpa samadhi* that must have been quite a letdown! There was no spiritual light; absolutely nothing. Finally, after three days, he saw a tiny point of light in the Christ center. He told me, 'I entered that light, and it gradually got bigger and bigger, until eventually it was infinite. And I was merged with that light. Now it doesn't make any difference anymore whether I have a body or no body; it is all the same to me.' "

†A great yogi's final, conscious exit from the body at the time of physical death.

Paramahansa Yogananda's hands are uplifted in blessing on his beloved disciple, on whom he had just bestowed *sannyas,* and the monastic name of Rajarsi Janakananda; SRF-YSS International Headquarters, Los Angeles, August 25, 1951.

"Then he said, *'He is here.'* He wasn't referring to the Master's physical presence, but to his omnipresent spiritual presence. *Just feel and receive.'* As he said these words a wave of divine power flowed over the whole audience—a tremendous surge of spiritual upliftment—and no one could doubt that he was right: The Master is alive."

Passing of the Guru's Mantle

Mrinalini Mata has said: "In India there is the spiritual tradition called *guru-parampara*—that is, the custom wherein the guru bestows his mantle of spirituality and authority on his successor. In Self-Realization Fellowship this continuity is certainly there. We have seen its unmistakable evidence in our revered Rajarsi Janakananda and Sri Daya Mata.

MEANING OF NAME, "RAJARSI JANAKANANDA"

Rajarsi is a spiritual title meaning "royal rishi"; Janakananda means "the bliss of Janaka." Janaka was a great king as well as a fully Self-realized master of ancient India.

Shown above is a note jotted by Paramahansaji while he was explaining the meaning of the monastic title he bestowed on his beloved disciple. The Sanskrit word "Rajarsi" is composed of *rāja*, "king" + *ṛṣi*, "rishi, illumined saint or sage." (Sanskrit is traditionally written in the Devanagari script of fifty characters. In Western alphabets, the Sanskrit vowel *ṛ* is often transliterated as *ri* and the *ṣ* as *sh*. The pronunciation is as shown in Paramahansaji's handwritten phonetic spelling *Rajarshi*.)

Paramahansaji said: "For you, St. Lynn, I interpret this title as 'king of the saints.'"

An early misspelling as "Rajasi," in which the *ṛ* in *ṛṣi* (rishi) is dropped, means "in the quality of *rajas*," the activating force in Nature; and is also the name of an aspect of the Divine Mother, God's creative or "activating force" in Nature. Neither of these definitions is related to the meaning of the spiritual title given by Paramahansaji to Rajarsi and penned by him as deriving from *rāja* (king) and *ṛṣi* (saint).

"I well remember the period shortly after Master left his body. Rajarsi was in such a sublime state of consciousness. So many times Master's presence became manifest in Rajarsi's body. On those occasions, Rajarsi's whole personality was gone, and it was just Master in that form. The little ways of gesturing that were so uniquely characteristic of Master, the special touch of his hand in blessing, the unusual expressions of speech and the quaint names that he had used privately with individual devotees—these we now saw expressing through Rajarsi, things Rajarsi had never done before."

Yogacharya J. M. Cuaron, disciple of Paramahansa Yogananda and leader of Self-Realization Fellowship Centers in Mexico until his passing in 1967, wrote the following shortly after Rajarsi's passing: "Last year, when I visited Encinitas, Rajarsi called me three times to his apartment to meditate with him and to give me his blessings. On these occasions he would pat my hand and head in the same way that Master used to do, with the same gestures and expressions. I hardly knew whether it were Rajarsi or Master sitting before me."

Rajarsi's oneness in Spirit with Paramahansaji enabled him to demonstrate for all future generations of disciples that a true guru is ever living; his blessings, guidance, and spiritual help are not limited by one brief span on earth or residence in a physical form. Speaking to Self-Realization monastics at Christmas 1953, Rajarsi gave the following beautiful testimony to the eternal relationship between a true guru and disciples who keep inwardly in tune with him:

> One does not realize how much he changes as he proceeds along the spiritual path. After I met Master in 1932 I felt changed a great deal; but when he would say to me, "I am in you, and you are in me," I did not quite know what he meant. But now I feel the presence of Master within and around me. Indeed, I am not aware of myself anymore! All I can feel is Master.
>
> The love of God is the only Reality. We must realize this love of God—so great, so joyful, I could not even begin to tell you how great it is! People in the world think, "I do this, I enjoy that." Yet whatever they are doing and enjoying inevitably comes to an end. But the love and joy of God that I feel is without any end. One can never forget it once he has tasted it; it is so great he could never want anything else to take its place. What we all really want is the love of God. And you will have it when you attain deeper realization.

Rajarsi Janakananda with Prabhas Chandra Ghosh, cousin of Paramahansa Yogananda and vice president of Yogoda Satsanga Society of India; Encinitas, California, 1954. See poem on page 168.

The Great Ones come to bring people back to God. Jesus came to bring realization to all men. And similarly Master came to save us, to bring us back to God. What a blessing many of us possess, to have known Master in this country! But the physical form means little; it is the soul that matters. Master is here now in an even greater way than he was when in the body. It is our joy, our grace, that we can receive his divine vibrations through following the teachings of Self-Realization Fellowship.

Master is right here. When I close my eyes, Master comes! Receive this blessing of Master, this great light, so great! and Master's greatness in it. He will touch your soul. God is coming through Master to you. Such love! Such joy!

You and I Are Free Forever

Written by Paramahansa Yogananda to Rajarsi Janakananda, May 5, 1949, expressing the divine unity experienced by their souls in their common realization of Spirit. The Guru often called this saintly disciple "Little One" in appreciation of his quiet humility.

My little one,
You and I are one
In Mother Supreme
In Her Eternity's dream.
When this earth melts in the cosmic dust
And our bodies dissolve, as they must,
Still our souls as a blended starlet will shine
Forever, ever expanding in the Divine.

This life is not only a dream,
But a dream
That already has come and gone
In the Mind of the Divine One.
Thus do I behold
With Eternity's eyes of old
All our earthly business pressures
Scant successes, struggles, and nightmares
All already dissolved in Time's cosmic molten stream
Flowing from Her cosmic dream.

You and I,
Though nigh,
Are no more here
In this cosmic motion picture.
Since you are gone
There is no worry, struggle none:

Only to calmly remember
We dreamt our dream and now are with Her, only Her.

Dreams are disturbing and hard to take,
But each dreamer should dream half-awake.
Nightmares and beautiful dreams
Are true awhile, but never as they seem;
So good or bad, whatever be coming,
Remember you are dreaming, only dreaming.

 This dream lies that we are here,
  Prisoners of a clot of earth
  Chained to life and death
 While we are already free—everywhere.

  'Tis delusion that tells
   Salvation and freedom are far away;
  'Tis wisdom that knows we dwell
   In everlasting freedom now and always.

In wakefulness of *samadhi's* light
Forget all dreams of the cosmic night.
You and I are free forever
Now, e'en now, in the Cosmic Mother.
Where we are
No scratch of worries can ever come near.
You and I forever are
Shining in Her love's star.

MR. LYNN AND PARAMAHANSAJI, CHRISTMAS DAY, 1936

The photograph was taken at a banquet at Self-Realization Fellowship head-quarters, Los Angeles. Paramahansaji had just returned from a visit to India. Mr. Lynn is wearing two gifts from his Guru: a "Gandhi cap" and a long shawl from Kashmir.

Mr. Lynn said: "I revere India as the land whose saints developed the highest of all sciences—yoga, the techniques for soul-exploration.

"How grateful we should be to a people whose greatest men, down the centuries, have given their lives, have renounced everything else, in order to explore the divine potentialities in man! America is rich in material accomplishments. And India is rich in the wisdom of Spirit. A combination of the two will lead to an ideal world-civilization."

Words of Paramahansa Yogananda About Mr. Lynn (Rajarsi Janakananda)

The following is a letter to Mr. Lynn, written by Paramahansa Yogananda in Kansas City, February 27, 1932—a few weeks after their first meeting.

This is to bless you on behalf of Babaji, Lahiri Mahasaya, Sri Yukteswarji, and myself, for saving the work at a very critical period of its existence. There is rejoicing in the inner world, for you helped the Great Ones to choose you as their luminous instrument for spreading the great emancipating Yogoda Satsanga work in the human-divine way.

The Great Ones choose able, willing devotees on earth to deliver other men from ignorance and suffering. On your human life the immortals have put their invisible hands. Blessed you are, beyond human dreams. Yes, God and the Masters could employ miracles to create big temples, but that would not change souls. But when the Great Ones find a powerful human soul who makes an altar of his heart with goodness and good works, then they come there to dwell and to work goodness.

The Great Ones love to establish a temple of Spirit in true souls like you, that wisdom-hungry devotees may come there to feast on the divine manna. Rejoice, rejoice, rejoice; and I too rejoice that the Spirit has taken the flute of your life to play the divine song of Yogoda [Self-Realization] and to lure others, truant children, back to His home.

Let us set ablaze new altars of Self-realization all over America. Let us help to drive away all darkness in men. Let us leave spiritual footprints in this dream-life, which others may follow to get out of the bedlam of misery-making nightmares, on to the region where dark dreams dare not tread—where God's fountains of bliss play in ever new ways to enthrall us, and where we may satisfy all the beautiful desires and fancies of the human soul.

With my deepest love and covenant to be your friend forever—until, crossing the portals of finitude and incarnations, we reach the bosom of the Divine Friend and become one with Him.

You are the Hindu yogi of Himalayan hermitages of the past who was sent in this life as an American prince, a Western maharaja-yogi, to light the lamp of Yogoda in many groping hearts.

Paramahansa Yogananda wrote the following letter to Mr. Lynn; dated October 13, 1933, Indianapolis.

Most blessed, beloved, little one. I have been so intoxicated with the God in you, and with the remembrance of the pillar of light that we saw enveloping us during the meditation in Chicago, that I did not realize I have been so long in writing you. You have never before been so strongly present in me. (You are always with me now, so I can't miss you.) So vividly have I seen your soul, like a glimmering jewel and an ornament in God's omnipresence!

I have been most happy since the Lord sent such a one as you to look after His work with me. I was tired of hollowhearted people who wanted respect from me because of their riches. I shrink from people who expect me to appeal slavishly to them for funds to carry on this work for the world. I and my dear ones here at the Mt. Washington Center would rather go hungry than beg a crumb from anyone who thinks that the anchor of life is not God, but material possessions.

I do not try to write you often, as I see you in God. Just a little while ago a great infinite tide was tumbling about in my heart, and I saw you swimming steadfastly with me to His shore. You are more fortunate than a million earthly kings, for God has given you self-control and a deep willingness to meditate. He is steadily drawing you unto Him. The most destructive shaft of *maya*-delusion is unwillingness to meditate, and thus to prevent oneself from tuning in with God and guru.

* * * * *

While looking for a location on the coast suitable for an ashram-retreat, the Guru wrote the following to Mr. Lynn, in 1934, about the beautiful seacliff property in Encinitas that later became the site of the Self-Realization Fellowship Hermitage, Ashram, and Retreat (see page 38). From the words in this letter we understand that in 1934 Paramahansaji already knew that Rajarsi would spend his last years in California, meditating in quietude rather than becoming "entangled with the details of our organization."

Some day I know God will free you from your business life and then you could come there, free from the entanglements of an organization, and meditate on that sacred hill in complete ecstasy with God. When you are thus free, I would not want you to be entangled with the details of our organization. I would want you only to revel in the

Two Rare Flowers in Earth's Garden—Paramahansa Yogananda and James J. Lynn

Infinite. When you get a pension from the Divine Mother to retire from your business life, there will be no more work for you—only thinking, meditating, and talking with Her.

*   *   *   *   *

The following lines written by Paramahansaji to Mr. Lynn express something of their divine relationship. The last two paragraphs are beautifully prophetic.

In Plato's story of the two stallions, one stallion was turned heavenward; the other earthward. But you and I are both turned heavenward; both are pulling the chariot of this work to the goal of divine fulfillment. Both of us, directed by the Great Ones, are necessary to draw the vehicle to its goal. That God has given me the privilege to serve is my blessed good fortune. I want nothing; my only desire is that I may establish this work as a divine oasis where aspiring souls may quench their thirst.

When your bodily changes do not affect your hoard of acquired spiritual realizations and your love for God, know then that you have become firmly established in Him. At heart renounce everything, and realize that you are just playing a part in the intricate Cosmic Movie. You will then forget it as a dream. Our environment produces the delusion in us of the seeming importance of our present roles and our present tests. Rise above that temporal consciousness. So realize God within that He becomes the only environment, the only ambition, the only influence in your life. You must work just to please Him. Meditate to bring Him on the altar of peace. Bliss is the only altar where God comes. He does not accept any other invitation.

When you and I have fulfilled our mission on earth, we shall be released. Then we shall be free to stay in heaven or to come back here. When we are free we may take trips to earth to load our boats with shipwrecked souls and to bring them safely to the divine shores.

I write this now, as I see this vision as I sit on my roof* under the sunlight, encircled by the infinite. When you come to me in future, together we shall rejoice exultantly, merging as one in the Eternal Sea.

*   *   *   *   *

Extracts from a speech by Paramahansaji, January 3, 1937, Los Angeles, at

*See photograph of the roof on page 109.

On the lotus pool, grounds of SRF Hermitage, Encinitas, 1938. Yogananandaji said of Mr. Lynn: "In him, and in a number of others in the West, has been fulfilled a prophecy uttered by our great master, Babaji, who said: 'The vibrations of many spiritually seeking souls in the West come floodlike to me. I perceive potential saints in America and Europe, waiting to be awakened.'"

a banquet held in his honor to celebrate his return to America after a visit to India in 1935–36.

It is because of Mr. Lynn's great love for God that I have given him the title of "Saint." In him, and in a number of others in the West, has been fulfilled a prophecy uttered by our great master, Babaji* of India, who said in 1894: "The vibrations of many spiritually seeking souls in the West come floodlike to me. I perceive potential saints in America and Europe waiting to be awakened."

The love and friendship of St. Lynn, and the affection of many other wonderful souls, have brought me back to this country. I had thought I might not return here. All places are the same to me because they are filled with the omnipresent Spirit. When I close my eyes, I am with my Father; I don't know whether my body is in India or in America. But the love of these friends brought me back here again.

In friendship there is no compulsion. In all other human relationships there is some form of compulsion, but friendship is the natural and spontaneous gift of the heart. St. Lynn and I live in the greatest joy and friendship. What I had expected of him in spiritual development, he has more than fulfilled. He represents the best in American business principles as well as in universal spiritual principles.

In the Encinitas Hermitage, St. Lynn and I have been meditating day and night. I have a hard time even getting him to eat or sleep. In this country I have never before known such unity and friendship, such divine communion.

* * * * *

Extracts from a talk given by Paramahansaji at an SRF gathering, Los Angeles, California, January 18, 1940.

Of all the women I have met in America, I think the one who has found highest favor with God is Sister Gyanamata [1869–1951]. Of all the men I have met here, I think the one who has found the highest favor with God is St. Lynn.

St. Lynn, more than most of us, is busy with many large affairs. Still, he and I hardly ever talk business or worldly matters. We meditate together.

A businessman of his type is expert in weighing comparative values.

---

*Mahavatar Babaji, guru of Lahiri Mahasaya (see page 184).

By his own efforts he has enabled himself to judge fairly between the worth of mundane joys and the worth of spiritual joys. Most people think that money will bring happiness, but they have no correct standard of comparison. They have never explored the possibilities of soul happiness. All the joys they know about are physical, material, and mental joys. Of the blissful soul-realm they know nothing. If, like St. Lynn, they follow a scientific path, *Kriya Yoga,* that opens up the hitherto unknown route to the soul, all men will someday be able to declare: "Once I knew myself only as a body; now I know myself as Spirit."

Some people say: "The Western man cannot meditate." That is not true. I gave *Kriya Yoga* initiation to St. Lynn shortly after I had met him; and since then I have never seen him when he was not inwardly communing with God. It is that most beautiful part of his nature which I enjoy. Whatever the subjects of our conversation, our meetings always end in deep meditation.

I remember, for instance, an occasion in 1933. I went to Chicago to give a lecture at the Parliament of Religions that was a feature of the great World's Fair. St. Lynn left Kansas City at the same time in order to meet me in Chicago. But he came only to meditate with me. While millions of people poured into the city to see the wonders on display, St. Lynn never went near the Fair!

Everyone who takes the spiritual path seriously will find that *Kriya Yoga* will take him as far as he wants to go: to God Himself. The Lord has no favorites. To him who loves God, to him He surrenders. But He cannot be known except through communion. No matter how many good works you do; no matter how much service you render to humanity; no matter how vast your philanthropies—they are not enough. To know God, direct communion through meditation is necessary.

God is like a beautiful, highborn, inaccessible princess. Many men seek her hand in marriage and send her magnificent gifts. But the one who wins her does more than the others. By the exercise of long, patient ingenuity he succeeds in meeting her, and, finally, in convincing her of his eternal love.

The case is similar between the truth-seeker and God. No outward gestures, however grand, convince the Divine Great Lady that the devotee will die of unrequited love unless he can meet Her. That conviction may be conveyed to Her only face to face. *Kriya Yoga* is a sacred password that opens the door of the Palace and secures the longed-for audience.

*   *   *   *   *

The following is from a letter written by Paramahansaji to Mr. Lynn for his birthday—May 5, 1940.

This letter is written to tell you how much India and I appreciate the precious gift of the Father in your birth. You were born for the sake of world upliftment. The good that has passed, by your instrumentality, through the Self-Realization work is appreciated not only by India and by those who know you here but is also held in high approval by the Heavenly Father, the Masters, and my humble self. World opinion and fame are fleeting, but God's certificate of recognition of your goodness and good work is everlasting.

I especially appreciate your birthday; for, besides being a gift to the world, you are a personal gift from God to me of the highest, sincerest, and sweetest friendship. And this is my prayer: that in my eyes you stand higher and higher in esteem and love, becoming continuously more spiritually progressive, that I may ever relate the same to my Father—He who has delegated me on earth to usher you in love's chariot to His everlasting kingdom.

May your birthday be an everlasting beacon light of inspiration to spiritual seekers on earth and in the astral world hereafter. May your life become an inspiring model after whose ideal pattern spiritual aspirants of East and West will shape their own lives.

My soul expressed the above perception, for you on your birthday.

*   *   *   *   *

The following are excerpts from a speech given by Paramahansaji at an SRF gathering in Los Angeles on June 29, 1941.

I have accepted students in all stages of spiritual development and have tried earnestly to train many of them. Some have failed on the path, but a large number have fulfilled their promise to God. The extraordinarily fast progress toward emancipation shown by a few devotees, like Mr. Lynn, is a source of deep happiness to me. One moon gives more light than countless stars.

I know how religiously Mr. Lynn conducts his life. He doesn't drink or smoke. He follows a simple diet of vegetables and fruit juices. He leads a celibate life. He doesn't go to the movies. For recreation he sits on the grass and meditates on the Divine. His whole existence is an exalted one, even though he attends to heavy business duties and is required to travel extensively in connection with his business responsibilities. He has had many temptations thrown in his way, but he has not succumbed to them. He has felt that Joy within which is greater than anything the world can offer. "Lord, Thou art more tempting than any other temptation."

I am proud that in Mr. Lynn a Westerner has stepped forth to show the world the worth in daily life of Yoga training. Through him the lives of many, many men will be profoundly changed and turned toward God.

Paramahansaji and Mr. Lynn outside the SRF Hermitage in Encinitas, 1940. In his *Autobiography of a Yogi*, the Guru wrote: "An American businessman of endless responsibilities (as head of vast oil interests and as president of the world's largest reciprocal fire-insurance exchange), Mr. Lynn nevertheless finds time daily for long and deep *Kriya Yoga* meditation. Leading thus a balanced life, he has attained in *samadhi* the grace of unshakable peace."

Paramahansaji and Mr. Lynn have just risen from meditation (see page 31). The love shining in their eyes as they would gaze at each other was beautiful to behold. "How outstandingly great, outstandingly gracious, outstandingly kind he was!" Mr. Lynn said of his Guru.

Pulling Together the
Divine Chariot

*Extracts from Paramahansa Yogananda's personal letters to Rajarsi
Janakananda written during Paramahansaji's return visit to India via
Europe in 1935–36. On June 9, 1935, the Guru sailed from New York to
London, where he lectured. From there he and the disciples accompanying
him traveled by car through western Europe, Palestine, and Egypt; thence
by boat to India.*

This segment of correspondence reflects in a very special and significant way the soul-communion and spiritual relationship that existed
between Paramahansa Yogananda and Rajarsi Janakananda, the exalted disciple who played such a unique role in the Guru's work on
earth. Paramahansaji's letters to Rajarsi from this period express
something of the earliest years of their God-ordained work together.
Portions of the letters, understandably, would be regarded by Paramahansaji as strictly confidential, written not for the public but addressed
to the soul of his beloved *chela:* "You are the only one in the world
with whom I think aloud," he wrote to Rajarsi in his letter of November 16, 1935. Other portions, however, contain spiritual counsel and
insights of great value to all sincere seekers. Indeed, the world is rarely
vouchsafed even a glimpse of such unity of spirit—a divine friendship
in its loftiest and most sacred expression, bonded in the love of God
that incarnated these two exalted souls together for the liberation of the
disciple and for the disciple's assistance to the world mission of the
Guru. Without intruding unduly into the Guru's missives, the following extracts are offered as an inspiration for other aspiring devotees
who seek to uplift themselves into the joyous holy company of those
who commune with God.

These letters bore the salutation shown in the opening selection, and
were signed "Swami Yogananda" or simply "S. Yogananda" or "S.Y."
(having predated the bestowal and use of the title Paramahansa,
which he received from his Guru while in India).

Park Hotel Maximilian
Regensburg, Germany
July 18, 1935

Most Blessed Beloved One,

Yesterday I saw Therese Neumann.* Greatly impressed with her.
She is a saint all right. We communed. She has asked me to see her pas-
sion and vision of Christ, when she bleeds while in trance. She is genuine. She was not in Konnersreuth when I went there. I said, "This
never should have happened." Then a miracle happened, and God
led me to her. I was very happy. Oh, how I wish you were here with
me. You could have felt her saintly vibrations. I can't thank you in
words for making all of this possible for my book. A great share of my
virtue belongs to you. I have already given you that in your astral
bank of karma. The boys† were overwhelmed by her saintly childlike
influence. She has penny-sized, perfect square, scaly fresh-healed
wounds on the back of her hands and small ones inside the palms—
also on the breast and feet. She saw me against the orders of her
Church, which tries to hide her [for her own protection].‡ I am writing
a great deal about her. She is going to have the vision with Christ tomorrow, and I will be there with her, perceiving her experience. How
grand! Here she is, amongst millions, one who has not eaten in eight
years, fully healthy—in blooming health, and smiles, and God.

Remember, as Therese sees Christ as he was, so also by concen-
trating days on any saint, his whole life on earth can be perceived—
first in one's life, then actually seen. Concentrate on Lahiri Mahasaya
with your Guru; that is your way. You will perceive, then see them.

With unending love, ever yours.

---

*A full chapter in Paramahansaji's autobiography is devoted to his meeting with Therese
Neumann, the Catholic mystic from Konnersreuth, Bavaria, who bore the mystical
wounds of Jesus. Though the primary purpose of Paramahansaji's trip was to see his Guru,
he was also taking the opportunity to collect material on the saints of India and the West,
to be included in the book he was planning to write: *Autobiography of a Yogi.*

† C. Richard Wright traveled with Paramahansaji as his secretary; and Bradford Lewis (son
of Dr. and Mrs. M. W. Lewis) accompanied them during part of the European segment of
the trip. An elderly SRF student, Miss Ettie Bletsch, was also a member of the party.

‡ The bishop had ordered that she should see no one without permission.

P.S. Without auto* it would have been almost impossible to see Therese. Auto did a good work.

* * * * *

Hotel Tyrol
Innsbruck, Austria
1 a.m., July 20, 1935

All day driving, all night driving. It is late, but before I leave Austria I must write to you a few lines. We had a wondrous experience with Therese Neumann. She was in conscious trance, bleeding from her eyes and her left breast. All around her head were bleeding marks of the crown of thorns. Her hands and feet had clear nail marks, square wounds. I saw her in the vision watching Christ carrying the cross; and she talked to Peter for deserting Christ.

Oh, how I missed you. The journey though hazardous has started out very well. This experience would be very good for my book, for Therese is a genuine Western saint.

Ever go deeper into the corridor of Eternity, never looking back, never measuring your progress; race continuously, calmly—with calm speed progress on and on into the infinite, ever-expanding sphere of Joy. Every day live in Eternity, fearing nothing, expecting nothing, shirking nothing; God is the only goal. Swallow up life and death in eternal consciousness of God. Give my deepest blessings to yourself and the dear group.†

Ever yours.

* * * * *

---

* Rajarsi had generously provided the funds for a new Ford automobile to be used by Paramahansaji and his party throughout their travels in Europe, the Middle East, and India.

†The Self-Realization Fellowship meditation group in Kansas City that met for a time under the leadership of Rajarsi. See letter of June 17, 1936, page 111, in which Paramahansaji explains that he wanted Rajarsi to have this period of training in sharing his spirituality with others.

Hotel Schwanen an d. Rigi
Lucerne, Switzerland
July 21, 1935

Beholding yonder Alps and lakes flooded with sunshine and clouds, I am writing to you. God is spread over the ripples in the water and the cloud waves in the sea sky. Everything is singing; your spirit is here. You would have enjoyed this peace above all. Occasional church bells, patter of feet, and a motorboat's sputter—and the silent song of the scenery. Everything is green-gold. I feel very sad and selfish to have traveled and seen all these without you, but it is only the call of duty (love for my Guru and for God's work) that made me undertake this journey. My supreme interest is in conversion of people. Many know English here, so this could be a good field.

Our illusion of being caged in the body is because we see it all the time and feel it—touch it, smell through it, taste through it, hear its noisy steps. Deny your confinement in the body. You are the whole tree of creation from which the flowers of stars and seas and leaves of created things are hanging. Body is one leaf of this tree, which is born and will fall off sometime. Recognize yourself as interested in everything of your whereabouts and yet not interested in everything. While you follow the routine and rules of the body, mentally neglect it as not of consequence. Body is the cage which bars the soul from flying out and feeling omnipresence. When you are conscious of your great body, the tree of creation, you will always be conscious of yourself, your great Self, and will not mind whether your little body is awake in life or falls asleep in death. However, your dear body has to do a great many things for leaving footprints of the Gurus and their teachings at Mt. Washington. You will be longer here on earth than I. I will remain as long [as God wills] until my work is finished. You have greatly helped in working out my destined task. A million blessings are yours.

Please write to me often. I shall send you many blessings of saints and communion with them. I don't need anybody now other than God, but I had one prayer to God: "I want to love Thee with all the love of true saints." That's why my interest is to see true saints on this trip and tell people how I felt. Those who drink God [the nectar of Bliss], they love to drink Him with those who love to drink Him.

Tell to the dear group, my spirit is with you all, ever meditating, silently watching and praying just behind the screens of your souls.

Ever be watchful and continuously careful to deepen your joy and contact with God.

I remain very sincerely yours.

* * * * *

Hotel Internazionale
Brindisi, Italy
July 28, 1935

Here we came after a long episode. My life is strange—always victory and defeat mixed together; only victory comes as a surprise from God in the end. In the meantime the forces of evil try to torture me. I wrote you from Rome about the auto's broken cylinder head, which had faulty [and costly] repairs at Venice. After several miles of travel [toward Rome] we fortunately returned to Venice to adjust the brakes. Then who should be shown but I, who am not a mechanic, a tiny spot on the repaired place. We had a terrible battle with the garage boss. We threw the motor into action, and water started to come out as small drops; and yet the mechanic denied any problem. At last they returned our money. Were we pleased! But think of all-night drive with water dripping, Dick filling it almost every hour.

In the morning we reached Assisi. There we saw St. Clare's tomb. St. Clare was a great devotee of St. Francis....Only after great request, he once broke bread with St. Clare; and while they were sitting together, people saw the church was afire. When they came, the fire vanished; it was the light of God....

St. Francis met Jesus in the woods almost every night. As I was visiting his living tomb and put my head on the shrine step, St. Francis appeared to me. Then I saw a tunnel of Eternity in which he disappeared. The entire cellar beneath the church was replete with his vibrations. You would have enjoyed very much to meditate here. St. Francis is one of my loved saints with whom I commune and have communed. I write to you these sacred things for God has made you sacred by meditation.

Blessed one, after leaving Assisi we came to Rome with the leaking cylinder head, now leaking profusely; Ford garage did wonders. Besides, we found the whole body stripped away from the spring due to heavy load; shock absorbers rubbed a big hole into the frame (nothing serious at all).

At Rome* we saw where Raphael (one of the world's greatest artists) was buried; where Caesar was stabbed; world's grandest church in the Vatican where St. Peter was buried—I got some of his vibrations, but not so strong as those of St. Francis in Assisi—here we saw the most wonderful pictures in mosaic. And all this without you in person; it is almost heartbreaking. I know, though you wouldn't like protracted sightseeing, you would enjoy meditating in the aromatic temples and churches. We saw the wood from Christ's crib, and the steps on which he walked when led to trial.

Then we left for Pompeii and Vesuvius. From childhood, it was something I dreamed of seeing; and who should materialize my dreams but you. We got a coin embedded in a piece of molten lava for you. This place is quite unique. You could see here melted earth; and how tons of it had spurted from this volcanic furnace of unimaginable heat— molten bricks thrown out. Here you could see how the earth was condensed out of gas into liquid, how liquid was solidified into the earth's crust, and then this molten lava changes from crust to solid stone. I have collected all stages of lava to rock formation. This is very interesting from the point of view of science and metaphysics of creation. Seeing Vesuvius one can readily see how this world was made in a furnace of heat, then cooled off, watered, and grass grown and humans put thereon for habitation....

Now I wish, as so many times I felt, that I had gone to India first. But summer keeps Europe at its best, and India in worst heat, which Dick and others perhaps couldn't have stood. Dick is somewhat frail and I shall be happy when I return him to U.S.A. safely. I am rather concerned about his health in India, though he is perfectly well now. He sends you his best regards.

Whenever you desire to commune with any saint, think first of his

---

* From Rome, Paramahansaji wrote on July 24: "Newspapermen interviewed me. All about work in best Roman papers expected tomorrow; but public meeting did not come through because of short notice. But I must come back in fall to give lecture. I am sure of a great following here."

image in the spiritual eye, then relax and concentrate in the heart, trying to feel some of his main characteristics. For instance, of Swami Shankara, think of wisdom; of Lahiri Mahasaya, a joyous perception and wisdom and devotion; of Yogananda, joyous perception and wisdom and devotion; of Sri Yukteswarji, wisdom and calm perception of bliss. Then lose yourself in the perception, and the soul of those individuals will possess you. You will act, reason, think, feel like them. Sometimes this might last for hours or days. When this is perfected, ultimately you will see them with closed eyes. When that can be done at will, you will see them with open eyes. This is the mystery of inner communion with saints. Practice that with unfailing zeal until you are certain of this communion.

I often feel your presence and see you. I am with you always, ever going deeper, ever feeling deeper bliss in you and in your devoted group and in me and all. Own the kingdom of immortality forever and forever.

With unending love, ever yours.

P.S. Life is strange. We are here, and we are here not; we meet and we part. Why we meet and why we part very few people know. Life comes from the invisible like a visible river; we are the bubbles in it. Then it ends in the invisible; the bubbles melt in the invisible. God alone has the key to this great secret. In the meantime we must patiently wait, for all will be well in the end.

* * * * *

Hotel New Angleterre
Athens
July 31, 1935

Would you believe now that we are in Greece. We are very glad after a race along hundreds of miles of mountainous roads. Even though we missed a boat, we found another lovely one; and after seeing the ruins and temples dating B.C., we are leaving for very dear Jerusalem —tomorrow—where I hope to see Jesus as he was. What a thrill. I am taking your soul with me to every spiritual place. Your soul and I meditate in every spiritual place I meet.

Half of my spiritual realization is yours. I have given so much to none but you. On your last day on this earth, [as] you feel a sudden illumination—a doubling of all your inner perceptions, an unexpected expansion, untold increase of Light and Bliss—then you will know what I have given to you. What I give you now is subtly added to the results of your own efforts. I have taken almost all of your karma on myself—and I will work the sufferance out in this body—that you may be free from the subtle traps of desires and attachments and have a clear sailing, like a shooting star in the distant heavens. [As a result] of all my efforts, you have been blest with ever-increasing joy and spiritual development without interruption. This is my spontaneous gift of my deepest love to you, which you have acquired with utter unselfishness, love, and devotion, and relieving me of a great many organizational duties. These are all very sacred things I am telling you.

Millions of madmen are rushing down the valley of death, skirmishing in the froth of ignorance. How few will understand what I say. Only true devotees know the glory of God and are in the joy of living in it. Those who sink in ignorance, they sink deeper. Those who climb higher, up and up they go until they reach a place from where there is no falling.

How important sometimes we think ourselves. Yet when the most important man is dead, creating a lot of hue and cry, still the world goes laughing by. This I am thinking of Mt. Washington without me. The *danse macabre* of *maya* must be conquered.

Delusion sings:

My ways are too subtle; that's why most succumb to my wiles.
I come, taking any guise, to lure souls to their doom.
The one who knows me today, from him I stay away.
Catching me, almost detecting my honeyed poisonous way—
Still they know me not yet.

This *maya* is very difficult to conquer; but with the help of God and Guru, all things are possible. Blessed you are, enjoying the protection of your own vigilance and the guarding of the gods. My soul and Lahiri Mahasaya are always with you, leading you on the eternal path.

Lahiri Mahasaya is my astral guru. (Very few in the world know this.)* From my childhood and before, he has definitely taken care of

* These words were addressed to Rajarsi before Paramahansaji had written *Autobiogra-*

me. It was through his wishes that I met Swami Sri Yukteswarji, my earthly guru. Once when I was dying in childhood, Lahiri Mahasaya came to me and healed me. I never have forgotten that.

One-pointedness of devotion and study—meditation, yoga, devotional contact of the Gurus—that's all that is necessary for positive salvation. Those that are unsettled, they die because of doubts or some other excuse which they create to stay away from God. Go deeper and deeper, never stopping, no matter how deep is the meditation. Never take for granted that any perception of God is the highest. God is immeasurable. I was deceived many times by fixing a standard of deep meditation. When I broke all measuring perceptions, I became endlessly blest; and being endlessly happy, am endlessly enjoying Him. Never do I expect to finish my perceptions about Him. No one can. Gita says: "Whose end even the greatest of all sages do not know, to Him we bow again and again." It is not necessary to know how big is the Lake of Sweetness as long as we can quench our mortal thirst with its nectar waters.

With deepest blessings. Endless love to you. Ever yours.

P.S. Emphasize and expand the best side of Mt. Washington with your light, dispelling any negativeness or shortcoming if it exists there.

*   *   *   *   *

Majestic Hotel
Jerusalem
August 9, 1935

There are no words adequate enough to express to you the joy and the vision and the blessedness which I perceived here. All the primitive atmosphere, the ancient background, is still present, marred only by a few modern buildings and hotels. His name is alive as before; only the Jesus that was and walked and suffered in the streets of Jerusalem very few people see. He was with me everywhere; and a very special

---

phy of a Yogi, in which he chronicled the life of his guru Sri Yukteswar (still incarnate when this letter was written) and of his *paramguru* Lahiri Mahasaya who, though he had left this earth, had ever reached down from the heavenly astral realms to bless Yoganandaji's life. *(Publisher's Note)*

communion I had in Bethlehem where he was born as the little babe body of Jesus. He touched me as I entered the ancient menagerie where Mary brought him into the world—in a humble little stable under an inn. This place is absolutely authentic. I know it from the Divine. But there are other places where different factions have marked Jesus did this and that, which have some errors. Every place was verified from within. Most places are authentic.

There are fourteen stations of Jesus' journey with the cross, where he was condemned, and ultimately where he was crucified, his body laid in the tomb, then ascended. I saw the hill where Jesus was tempted by Satan; where he was entertained by Mary and Martha; and Mt. of Olives gave me the greatest vision and inspiration where Jesus was received up into heaven. There is a mark in the rock which retains his footprints. Sometime, when I write elaborately, I want you to read that; I don't want to mar the continuity of the charming experience by writing choppy information.

Thank God and you His great instrument through which it was possible for me to stay here three days and three nights. It was a continuous blessed experience.

The Jerusalem you have found within is your omnipresent consciousness, and the Christ-bliss is the Jesus which is risen within you after being crucified by the Satan of ignorance. Your life would be happier not in travels but in meditation, in retirement, and occasional communion with devoted students and devotees. My life is used to both travel and staying in one place. I prefer the latter; only because students of former incarnations cannot come to me where I am, that's why I have to travel from India to America and from there to other places.

Last night God told in a clear voice to one Arabian Christian minister (who is trying to unite Christian sects into one) to come to me. We had met on the street, and he recognized me according to divine direction. He accosted me in a broken English; and my guide dissuaded him, thinking he was trying to beg some money. Then when I came back to the hotel today, he was staying there without knowing I was there too. And just as we were packing—to leave very early in the morning to cross the desert into Egypt—he came to me in this hotel, knelt down, and delivered the message he received from God, and asked to be initiated. I showed him the light, and he went wild with joy. Indescribable was his happiness. He cried that I always include him in my prayers. Aren't you glad to see how God is preaching through me now? I like that way much better than lecturing to people drawn only by advertising. Krishna said that out of one thousand one seeks me; and out of one thousand that seek me, one knows me. The last part of my life will not be lecturing, but only teaching those that God sends to me. I seek no disciples, no fame, no organization, no crowds, nothing but God, God, God, and the Gurus in God. The Arabian Christian after initiation said, "I am your first disciple in Jerusalem." I replied, "I am glad God sent you to me."

You have satisfied all my desires for an ideal beloved one who has carried out all the demands of divine discipline. What more could I want? I pray many pattern their lives after you; it would be worthwhile for those who would be saved through your example. One moon gives more light than all the stars....

It is 11 p.m. The message went around the hotel, and a host of people came to be blessed just as I was writing to you. I am deeply touched to see what faith Christ has given to those Arabian converts. Christ's work is living in many souls; and I am so thrilled to see God send so many souls to me, without my seeking them, to be blessed in Him. Tears well up in my eyes. I am leaving the Holy Land at 3 a.m. with the greatest proof of Christ's power.

Whatever comes to you, good or bad, remember all will be turned to good if you see God always and refuse to acknowledge the power of evil or trouble. His hand can be seen through all the openings of contradictory events.

With love eternal, yours.

* * * * *

Bombay, India
August 24, 1935

I write to you regularly no matter if it is 1 a.m. or 3 p.m., and I certainly do miss your letters. Perhaps you are very busy, but you don't have to write much; write a few lines, but write regularly.

Little could we imagine [effect of] the London publicity. Whatever goes in London, goes in India. All the important newspapers through Associated Press have written two columns, practically a summary of my London lecture in all important Indian papers; and I am now known all over India. I was received in Bombay by prominent citizens, heavily garlanded and showered with flowers. All this glory belongs to Lahiri Mahasaya and Guru.

Guruji didn't write to me in Port Said, but his letter was waiting here: "I am overjoyed, extremely delighted that you are here. It will soothe my eyes seeing you and your disciples. Motor from Calcutta to Serampore and take me with you." Now this is very unusual for him to express such joy and request. He is so austere and undemonstrative, and almost never requests anything for himself. And think, you have given all this joy not only to me but to Guruji. My earthly father and Calcutta are making big preparations to receive us at Calcutta Howrah Station. We have to take the train because the roads have been flooded due to monsoon. Besides, we have to see Mahatma Gandhiji at Wardha, which is a great jungle-way for motor cars. We start today for Wardha, Wednesday morning reaching Howrah 19th August at 6 o'clock. A reception committee and newspaper reporters are going to receive us. I am very encouraged that the political movement has subsided and people are turning to spirituality. Dr. Nawle, who visited our hermitage at L.A. and has a center in Poona, wrote up about our work in all the papers. He is going to arrange campaigns in all big cities of India....

To be known by God is everything. Like Buddha who gave up everything, live only for God, Self-Realization Fellowship, and Guru's work; and you will attain everlastingness in heaven. Though it is hard to forget earthly difficulties, still remember this earthly life of yours is only to test your strength and sacrifice. Even though you are so harassed in business, cling to God and God's work to your utmost, in spite of difficulties, and you will attain. That is your supreme test for the realization you have attained in meditation.

Silence is a bottomless sea. Even in *nirbikalpa samadhi,* when one thinks he has reached the greatest depth, he has to go deeper and deeper still—not for a millennium or two, but eternally. And when he declares, "I know that the ever new joy of God is unendingly ever increasing," then the devotee reaches finality. Realize this and never look for the endless end but seek it endlessly and you will reach finality.

Tender my deepest blessings to the divine group and measureless love to you.

Boundless blessings. Very sincerely ever and ever.

Ghosh's College of Physical Education
Calcutta, India
September 19, 1935

Words fail to describe that I have such a one who is helping me to spread the victorious army of God in this sacred land. When comes such another—a comrade sent by God to battle for His work and spread His sacred name.

Told you by airmail we were laden with garlands at Bombay; stayed with the austere man of complete renunciation, Mahatma Gandhi, at Wardha. His English disciple Madeleine Slade (daughter of an English admiral) undergoes same discipline very cheerfully; such renunciation is hardly to be seen. They clean latrines every morning for the villagers.... Mahatma is admirably sincere, unusually sincere; cornered he admits any shortcoming. After great discussions, he took lessons (*Kriya* and recharging exercises from me). His secretary Mahadev Desai and many others took lessons. I and Dick sat by the Mahatma; he gave food on my plate with his own spoon. Mahatma has promised to practice lessons for at least six years, and tell me then what he thinks of them. The secretary is very self-sacrificing. I was invited to talk in Hindi to a packed town hall (people sitting in windows). London campaign did the work; our work is known everywhere in India.

When I arrived at Calcutta, we couldn't get out of the train because of the crowds. I wished you were with us. Maharaja of Kasimbazar (son of the late Maharaja who helped me start Ranchi school) and hundreds of others received us with countless garlands, a Rolls Royce and a fleet of autos and motorcycles (ridden by my Ranchi students). My brother Bishnu Ghosh, to whom I taught recharging exercises at Ranchi school, has kept my name alive and has built 400 strong athletes. I daresay you never saw such prime of youth, as if their bodies were made in a factory. My brother has done what I wanted to do. His disciples have gone all over India starting [yoga] health centers; he is famous throughout India. And now Bishnu has brought all these youths for spiritual training. We are going to do real unprecedented work here.

I was busy in America, but I did not imagine completely what work was waiting for me here. Hundreds visiting me, clamoring for lessons. I am busy from morning till one o'clock at night. I am bound hand and foot with the love of people, initiations, songs, and meditations. Oh, such spiritual atmosphere I so long missed; day and night passes with God, and God-mad, God-hungry crowds. Flowers and fruits of all descriptions are presented to me; people from all parts of Bengal and India are pouring in. I got invitation from Madras to speak; but for now I have enough work in dear Bengal.

Visited my great Master Sri Yukteswarji first time. We flew into each other's arms and remained there in sobs for long. (We are staying at Father's. Father and I embraced each other and remained that way for long, crying.) Such joy you have given. I have shown your picture to Master—and to all—and his and thousands of blessings are being sent to you through the air. They all know what you have meant to me and the work. I am sending you a souvenir from Master—he is giving especially to you a piece of his wearing apparel.

I forgot to tell you what joy it was to receive your second letter. I am sorry I did not make it clear where you could reach me. Your joys are everything to me. Your letters are extremely delightful and encouraging. You and I are harnessed to the Divine Chariot, and I must constantly keep sight of you while I am covering God's territory. You won't believe what tremendous work I have to do here. Now the time is ripe as there is a lull in political work and people have once more turned to God for light, so becoming of India.

Went to Ranchi for seven days, spoke to thousands; spoke to thousands here…. I wish I could show you what is going on. The time is at hand. All India is ready for our teaching…newspapers report anything I say.

For what you have already done, a million thanks. I broadcast your name to all saints; they are blessing you.

Ever yours.

* * * * *

Calcutta, India
September 26, 1935

Today is festival day. Master honored us with his presence in the procession, which toured the city. This procession had a Yogoda Satsanga flag, and it was accompanied by musical instruments (drum and cymbal) like you have seen and heard played at the [Mt. Washington] headquarters.

Everyone knows you here and is blessing you for the temple you are helping to create. How well God directed me to ask you about the temple, for everybody expected it. It is a wonderful exchange: India sent the life-giving work to America, and she sent a temple here.* Thousands are gathering to cooperate with the cause and spread it the length and breadth of India. I held my first class in Ranchi; I am going to hold a yoga class next Sunday....I am day and night busy interesting people and looking for the house and garden for a center.

I was overjoyed to receive your first letter in Calcutta. My father and also my Master send you blessings. My father recovered from his severe illness, but is barely living; somehow body and soul together.

How to build the soul's future mansion? Every good action leaves a good residual thought in the brain. Sometimes these thoughts are seen as good dreams, visions. The good dreams or visions are the glimpses of what the soul could permanently materialize in the astral world. Each good soul after death can take life force from his developed being and the ether and materialize a mansion and scenery in the etheric land that would change shapes and take ideal and permanent form after the wishes of his heart. In this self-created permanent pranic mansion, the soul dwells with other kindred-spirit devotees, and worships God as light, and studies the mysteries of the astral land. Weak souls haven't this privilege. Hence, students who learn to control life force now, and who meditate more and see true visions, can be astral architects after death and build their mansions in heaven.

After life on earth, life must be experienced in the astral world where all things are carried on by will and energy. After experiencing life and longevity in the astral world, which may extend from one to several hundred years, one learns by great methods from the guru to be ready for the lightless lightsome, darkless darksome, joyous joysome land of pure Spirit. This is a very secret truth I have told you and the divine group.

---

* Before leaving the U. S. for India, Paramahansaji had asked donations from his Western students and friends in order to establish a temple in Calcutta. As he explains in his letter to Rajarsi dated October 18, 1935 (see page 84), the donations, which were sent to him in India, were ultimately used to purchase the property in Ranchi where the Guru had founded a school in 1918. A plaque on the veranda of the Ranchi administration building gratefully records the names of those disciples who contributed, chief among whom was Rajarsi.

Swami Sri Yukteswar and Paramahansa Yogananda in religious procession, Calcutta, September 26, 1935. (At right is C. Richard Wright, Sri Yogananda's secretary.)

Be up and doing; never forget God and calmness for one moment. Become the sea of joy, untouched by the wave of activity passing over you. If only you were here in such atmosphere of spiritual encouragement. Day and night is passing in joy. God's name is everywhere. Hungry devotees, mostly men and boys, coming from all directions to drink truth from the well in me. It is grand. I am afraid that but for you I never would, and never could, leave India. I am, it seems, through with everything but God and His devotees. God has taken away everything; I am swimming in His holy Name, the holy atmosphere of *Aum,* of Joy. India is richest in spite of her poverty.

All my love to you, beloved of my soul.

Very sincerely yours.

* * * * *

Calcutta, India
October 1, 1935

Well, I am more busy than I was in America. I am literally swamped with people seeking healing and initiation. Never in the history of India yoga has been taught to as large a class as I had. The audience in most lectures ranges from 1,000 to 2,000; and it is steadily growing. What good you have done sending me here, you will never know. The newspapers are very sympathetic toward me and the work, and my writings are being printed in the associated papers in India. I am getting lecture invitations from all over India. I am lecturing all over Calcutta and getting tremendous response. Our yearly festivity passed off very smoothly; we had an enormous crowd, and eight hundred people were fed. In the morning, we had religious festival in which Swami Sri Yukteswarji was present. He was photographed with the procession.

Dear one, I cannot tell it in words, the feeling you have created between Calcutta, India, and America. I am pleased to see that hundreds are receiving instructions, and I am surrounded by dozens of finest boys of Bengal who are meditating with me. You would have been engrossed in this deepest atmosphere of devotion, which I so long missed. I am happy with a little food at noon, and all day and practically all night I am working—then mostly meditating in this divine at-

mosphere. Material worries and responsibilities and years of financial
struggles had caused a subconscious dread, from which only God freed
me through your advent and divine cooperation. Here I feel free. The
Himalayan caves are calling me and the peoples' heart-caves are welcoming me. I am establishing His temple in the souls of men. It is
wonderful to work amidst people who don't need coaxing to be spiritual. But for you and a few others I would certainly have no attraction
to go back [to the West], even if I were lord of many hermitages. India
with all her poverty and material sickness is far the richest in spirituality. In India, ever since I landed…all I have heard is of God. Dick is
tasting this fine spiritual atmosphere and now realizes that of which I
used to so much tell him in America.…Under this divine atmosphere
he has been steadily improving spiritually. A million times I have
wished you were here in this spiritual paradise; I wish the dear group
of Kansas City and Mt. Washington were here to drink from the nectar ocean of the spiritual atmosphere of India. Your dear picture is
blessed by Master and all. The piece of cloth I sent you was specially
blessed by Swami Sri Yukteswarji.

I am meeting great saints. I was in Mahatma Gandhi's *ashrama,* and
you will be surprised to hear he was childlike, and divine enough to
take initiation from me. Many others, including his secretary Mahadev Desai, took lessons from me. I will tell you more later. One thing
I am beholding in India again is that the people here give the greatest
and primary interest in realizing God first. Dozens lie prostrate wherever I go, and are healed just by a mere touch because of their faith in
God through me.

The atmosphere you have created around you is prevalent in most
places in India and can be found at the slightest wish. People flock
around you, which encourages you to renounce all and climb towards
God. In the West, even in religious circles, unless you have money
[which says you are a success] few pay attention to you.

Blessed one, all you have renounced for God is reserved for you
manyfold in heaven, to be used in any incarnation you want. Those
who sacrifice wealth for God are never left poor in any incarnation; this
is the law.

I tell you how I am feeling now. The tremendous river of activity—
seeing people, talking, lecturing, moving, motoring, discussing—all
these are passing like waves over me, while I am the ocean of enjoy-

ment. I am telling many, I am walking with an ocean of joy tied in my breast with the strings of thoughts.

Every thought, every action—even desire—has become a temple of God. The great silent God is playing hide-and-seek with me. He is inexhaustible Joy, eternal food for the redeemed ones to enjoy untiringly throughout eternity. God's joy is ever new and ever newly entertaining. This keeps the redeemed prophet intoxicated and busy throughout eternity, precluding ever getting tired of God. This prevents also the cropping up of desires for change and consequent return to earth's shores. Think a few years hence, when you and I and a few others will close our trialsome play over earth's stage, what will be waiting for us. Eternal enjoyment, everlasting freedom. There will be no fear of injury to the body or calculating what food to eat, nor fear of losses, nor scanty wealth to do God's work. We will dive to the bottom of the ocean and swim with the fishes or soar with the winged balls of the Milky Way.

Last of all, I want you to know that many saints and myself are sending our richest loving vibrations to you and Mt. Washington. She [Mt. Washington] is going through trials, but God's grace and your instrumentality see us through. Dear one, because you have done so much and because of God and our supreme Guru's wish I ventured to bother you about completing this very great tour....All India is ripe for me, and I must lecture and hold classes in the principal cities and found and stabilize a temple-center with a correspondence course covering all of India.

Please accept my heartfelt love and give that to the very dear group; and remember, no words can repay for all you have done. All Bengal and India sends you loving greetings.

With eternal love.

I am ever yours.

P.S. Flowers from Swami Sri Yukteswarji's garland, which he wore on 26th of September morning Yogoda Satsanga festival, for you and a little for each member of the group to be saved in lockets.

* * * * *

Calcutta, India
October 9, 1935

I am sending you a letter a week. What bandits perpetrated political crimes in open daylight of public opinion. Mussolini is exercis-
ing his "heroism" on an ill-armed race and has assured glorious victory; why didn't he try his victorious schemes on France or some
other powerful race, then he would have faced some music. I am so
thoroughly disillusioned with him, that he is working his ambitions
on his own people at the cost of poor Abyssinia. He has mighty karma
to pay for attacking innocent people without provocation. I daresay
if Mussolini had to fight in the very first ranks he would not sanction
this war. Looks like Britain is taking precautions and does not like the
bland audacity of Italy.

It is now several months since I left the blessed shores of America;
I am beginning to miss her and you dreadfully. Now that I have seen
all these people, I am sorry [that I cannot be with] both the people of
America and India. I only wish America and India were nearer.

I am negotiating the buying of a twenty-acre fruit orchard with a dou-
ble-storied building....It is Master's last great wish to see the work established in a central place in India. That is why I am bending all my energy to create it with your benign help. I would be able to send future
American visitors to come and accept the hospitality of our India *ashrama,*
which you are helping me to create. For a time this place seemed lost to
us as another party was negotiating. I let it go without making any fuss,
but it looks like it may come back into our hands again.

It is very hot here, continuous humidity in summer, the fan has to
go day and night; but approaching winter would be very pleasant. I am
again, shortly, going to Ranchi to see what I could do there. If I can
save the Ranchi property, it would be saving a great school. I told Maharaja to incorporate it in [Yogoda] Satsanga's name and endow it, but
he kept putting it off. Now he is dead, leaving it to the fates and the
gods and public pity. This has stirred my soul; I will do what is best.
There are many ways of doing this; and if by grace of God the Calcutta
headquarters is established and Ranchi saved, you would have helped
me to do two greatest things in India.

I often see you dazzling in the dark expanse of the Infinite Bosom.

After millenniums of floating, the bubbles of our lives have met together to meditate in the eternal safety of the Ocean which holds us. So long we were drifting, afraid of the storms and trials and buffeting of incarnations. I am walking with that Ocean locked in my breast. I am walking with the entire sky bottled up within my mind. I am forgetting in what body I am. I am working in you, and I am working in Yogananda, and in the group. I am working in everything. How then can I cease working or find redemption from work? I can sleep, and I can work forgetting myself while working. That is a way, don't you see, to escape the consciousness of working. I can hear carping criticism with as much equal joy as praise. I am in the praising and the criticizing voice; I am both voices. They are unutterable without me.

One thing very hard to overcome is the consciousness of "now." The past is dimmed, the future obscure. But today is intoxicating us with infinite illusions. Today we are men with various duties, unending struggles, states of our health, hard-battling moods, die-hard habits, formidable difficulties, present circles of friends and family. All these will certainly change, or we will be transferred from this life sooner or later. Still we refuse to recognize the utter fickleness of our environments. This very pen with which I write, somebody else will also use for some other purpose. I see this; but it is not exactly realized by the "now consciousness." This "now attachment" is the cause of the greatest delusion.

Do your duties now without being attached to them now or anytime hereafter. Test yourself every minute if you are doing your duty without attachment, just to please God. Mentally every day renounce everything; then when the real day of renouncement comes, you won't have to feel surprised. You are now in charge of Kansas City properties and Mt. Washington Estates. You are working for these just to please God. When complete detachment comes [at the end of life], one is pleased only when his earthly charges and possessions and all were used to do lasting work for God. The man of God does not wish to hold anything for himself, but for God and His work only. So be your consciousness in reality, that you test your meditation-attained joy in complete renunciation. Renunciation, mental detachment, is extremely necessary before one can acquire the vast Eternal Kingdom of God. Any consciousness of possession is a stumbling block against the possession of the Infinite Kingdom. The finite must be forsaken if the Infinite is to be possessed.

I can truthfully tell you I have renounced all. I don't know I own anything except God. I am happy beyond the dreams of kings. So are you happy, blessed prince-child of God. Lahiri Mahasaya is holding you in his lap; and I am holding you by the soul, tied with love's cords. Days are passing, and I keep on and on moving into the deeper spaces of divine perception; and there together forever we will swim in Him and ever-changing joy.

Please give my deepest blessings to yourself and the group, and tell them here beneath sultry skies and saint-besmeared atmosphere I wrote the above in God and send only what God feels necessary to tell you through me. I am the hands and mouth of God to tell you what He wants me to tell you.

With infinite love to you and the divine group, I remain very sincerely yours.

*   *   *   *   *

Calcutta, India
October 18, 1935

In my last letter I told you of the Calcutta property and how though we liked it, it slipped out of our hands. Nothing better could happen— something unexpected, unprecedented—for I have succeeded in persuading the new Maharaja of Kasimbazar to sell me the Ranchi school, my first creation. This is sixty-five acres of land with four hundred mango trees, six hundred guava trees, and also litchi trees, extensive playgrounds, palatial buildings. Ranchi is the best climate, next to Los Angeles. No humidity. The English governor lives in this area eight months of the year. There are many English missions here. Now we will have a headquarters of Yogoda Satsanga (Self-Realization Fellowship) which will be most unique in the history of our organization....Here at Ranchi will be the headquarters of Yogoda Satsanga and our mission (Shyama Charan Lahiri Mahasaya Mission) with three departments. (1) The Brahmacharya school (school of discipline for boys); (2) correspondence course [*Yogoda Lessons*]; (3) service department for helping the poor and sick in the villages. Here everybody can work and create in this divine climate. After everything grows here, we will create a center in Calcutta....*

So, dear one, I feel your helping me here is more than amply re-warded; I feel glorified for being able to come to India, just to be able to accomplish this....My life's dream of eighteen years is fulfilled. You saved and freed Mt. Washington, and now you have been the savior of the India-known Ranchi school. Hail true child of God! You now stand the beloved figure of Hindu hearts who know about you, and will know in the future....

I am sitting in front of a window. I see life force lifting and flapping the wings of sparrows, and in the flowing wind, and in the moving leaves, and in the white blue sky, and in the layers of brick walls, and in the bone and flesh cells of my body. The white sky, the cream-colored houses, the brown bodies, the green trees, the grey sparrows, are different vibrations of the same life force. Oh, what magic light with so many changing variations! When you look at anything, look at it steadily until your inner light comes out and drowns that object, and then you will see that object transformed into life force. This is a new way of converting solids, liquid lakes, and skies into the light of life force. Solids have dimensions and hardness—it is condensed life force that vibrates dimensions and hardness. The worldly man experi-ences the world as walking on solids, swimming in water, flying in the clouds. The yogi must feel himself moving in light; for the body is light, and all is light. Forsake human habits; utilize your Self-realization to cultivate yogi-habits and God-habits. Yogis walk in light; feel and see the body as light. The world is not the same as the world perceives it. The yogi must perceive the world as a bundle of sensations springing from the different variations of life force. So, dear one, perceive the world now as a motion picture on the screen of your consciousness and the sky.

With my love and the love of all Bengal and India, and the bless-ings of Gurus, I remain very sincerely yours.

P.S. I am invited by the Maharaja of Orissa to pass some time in his

---

* In 1939, Paramahansaji acquired a large estate property at Dakshineswar on the Ganges, four miles from Calcutta. This became Yogoda Math, the official registered administra-tive headquarters of Yogoda Satsanga Society of India. Ranchi continued to be the hub of many YSS schools, the mailing of *Yogoda Lessons,* correspondence with YSS members,

palace at Puri, and the Maharaja of Mysore has invited me to his palace. Starting there soon; will be back here soon. I am swamped with invitations. Great work is being accomplished. Many prominent people taking lessons.

Ever yours.

* * * * *

Calcutta India
October 25, 1935

Several mails (weekend mails) have gone by without your dear letters, however I know God is with you and protecting you evermore. Joy knows no bound that during my lifetime with your divine instrumentality I have seen the headquarters at Mt. Washington and the Eastern headquarters at Ranchi free and clear. I am free, I am happy; may the Divine Being and the Gurus give you the same satisfaction and freedom in your business and everything....Thousands of blessings of saints, friends, and well-wishers are pouring on me, all of which I turn over to you for being the divine instrument. I am sending snapshots of a view of the Ranchi garden. Here you must come sometime, then you will see what has been accomplished....

The more I see the miseries of the world and rebel against Nature's cruelty, the more God shows me this world is a dream. Then and then only I find justification for all the tragedies of this earth, which otherwise are absolutely inexplicable. People are crying, laughing, wanting, in the sleep of delusion; only wakefulness in God is the remedy for all the invasion of dualities. Keep the mind always in one Bliss, then all dualities will vanish. Among all trials, moods, mental changes, worldly duties, keep the underlying mind floating in absolute Bliss and *Aum;* then you will understand this world to be a dream. Be of even mind in everything; then you will know this world to be a dream. Love all with the love of God; then you will know this life to be a dream. See one life in solid, liquid, gases, energy; then you will know this universe is made of a dream. Dreams are motion pictures of life force

a pilgrimage center for Convocations and other commemorative gatherings, and many other spiritual and humanitarian functions of Paramahansa Yogananda's society.

Sri Yogananda *(center)* and his secretary, C. Richard Wright *(right, seated),* in Ranchi, July 17, 1936. They are surrounded by teachers and students of Sri Yogananda's School for Aborigine Girls.

Sri Yogananda with teachers and students of Yogoda Satsanga Society school for boys, Ranchi, 1936. The school, founded by Yoganandaji, was moved to this site from Dihika, Bengal, in 1918, under the patronage of the Maharaja of Kasimbazar.

and mind. Mind makes the films and life materializes the pictures through the Divine Operator. Live in this world as if you are dreaming; think yourself awake only when you are meditating and enjoying Bliss.

My deepest blessings to the dear group at Kansas City, and tell them of the Self-Realization Fellowship happiest news about the headquarters in Ranchi, India.

With deepest love, ever yours.

P.S. Please write often.

*   *   *   *   *

The Palace
Bangalore, India
November 1, 1935

Here I am being royally entertained by His Highness Prince Yuvaraj (like Prince of Wales) of Mysore, the second largest free state in India. During Britain's occupation of India this is one of the free states left to rule itself; only a British resident (like an ambassador) stays here. The prince is hosting me in his palace and taking lessons from me. He is deeply interested and is talking of opening a center here. He has arranged for three public lectures followed by classes, which was never before undertaken in the history of Mysore. However, I am under no illusion of name or fame; all I want to do is to serve God first and then serve man with God. This "The Palace" is the summer capitol of Mysore. The prince Yuvaraj is also taking me to introduce me to his brother, His Highness the Maharaja of Mysore—the Maharaja being childless, his brother [the Yuvaraj] is heir to the throne. I am lecturing tonight on "Art of Living" in the high school; and on the last night, in town hall—seating 3,000, just newly erected—introduced by Mr. Chetty, the former Prime Minister of Mysore State who principally donated for this temple (alabaster town hall). This is one of the finest buildings in town. Mysore State is very advanced and is progressing after the pattern of western cities. My real tour in India has begun.

Ranchi mission is to be named "Shyama Charan Lahiri Mission."

This would be our first in establishing his name, as Vivekananda went back to India from U.S.A. and established Ramakrishna Mission. Buying of Ranchi has and is bringing blessings from Master and all. Everything is being well organized. Dear one, you have no idea what God has done through you....

I will complete my work here and in Europe and try to be with you all soon, God willing. Please bear with me as I am trying to do best not for myself but for the lasting glory of the work, and to carry out the wishes of Gurus, and to glorify you for all you have done. I would love to be meditating with you and the group.

I am sitting facing the beautiful palace grounds, only there are bars in the windows. A mass of bougainvillea flowers has proved to be the altar of God and the sunshine—what colors the astral cosmic light has lent it, out to the various shades of flowers and leaves and sky. I am moving in the wind; saturated in the blue heavens. My joy is the color of the flowers. Every blade of grass I feel as the hairs of my body; and I feel the sparrow picking at one of my grassy green hairs. How wonderful to love everything, not in a passing way but with deep concentration until love opens a portal into the Love which is everything. While you love nature, love deeply, so deeply that you lose yourself in that love, and you will perceive the Love which is in everything. You will feel nature, earth, and sky as your body and self. Love everything after *samadhi* and you will know the love aspect of God. This approach is important. Love all with the love of God. That love alone is pure.

With my love to you, I remain very sincerely yours.

* * * * *

The Palace
Bangalore, India
November 8, 1935

This is my short letter to say we are literally "idolized" here. The enclosed article will show. I am busy day and night. I had a class of almost five hundred. As the mail has to go, this will be my shortest letter, but will carry limitless love and blessings to you. Meditate deep and deeper; and when you think it is deepest, go deeper yet. Do this unto eternity, forgetting time and years, and you will stay there in God forever. More in my next letter. Mysore is won; this is very great for our work. With deepest love.

Ever yours.

* * * * *

The Palace
Bangalore, India
November 16, 1935

Blessed one, words cannot express my happiness to know that right along with all of your responsibilities you have freed our beloved Mt. Washington from practically all debts. What freedom you have given to the institution; may that freedom be yours in spirit and in material things. You have also helped me very greatly in acquiring my freedom from organizational work. After seeing Mt. Washington free and Ranchi head-quarters—Shyama Charan Lahiri Mission established I am glad beyond dreams. A thousand hermitages elsewhere would not have given so much joy as the salvaging of the tottering Ranchi Vidyalaya school. All India is pleased to see it stabilized and thanks you for it....I will go to Ranchi and organize matters there the best way I can, for I believe Ranchi has immense possibilities. Of course, this will prolong my stay in India in her most spiritual atmosphere; and I will have the opportunity to serve her after I have served America for sixteen years.

When I think of Los Angeles and you, I think of the newfound souls here; and when I think of missing them, I think of you all. I am in a great fix. But for you and perhaps a very few others there I would not return to America, for I do not like the financial struggles and high cost of living there. India is getting more that way, yet there is always great freedom to pursue the spiritual path; and spiritual people haven't to look after their personal needs. There is opportunity in almost every city for plain living and high thinking....

I am overjoyed to know you enjoyed the relic of Master's which I sent you, and that the group enjoyed possessing part of it. How I long sometimes to drop in suddenly near you, which I often do spiritually; and so often I feel your presence. There are very few in the world who do for God's work with the consciousness that you do. We own nothing in the world; we are given the use of things. Some are given material and some are given spiritual possessions; and even as the Heavenly Father gives us His things to use, so He expects us as willingly and freely to share our things with others. As God gives all He has, wealth and *samadhi,* to all those who demand, so when we, Buddha-like, share all with others we begin to become as God is.

It is easy to renounce everything in India, but I found it is harder to renounce everything in America as there is no encouragement, no provisions for spiritual teachers (most of whom are enslaved by salaries). Besides, the dread of poverty and fear of being left out is extremely emphasized. Plainness of living is deprecated and luxurious living encouraged. That is, cotton robes which I used to wear in public meeting in U.S.A. were severely criticized and silken robes extremely praised. Once in a hurry I wore my orange silk robe here and the papers criticized me about it and requested me to wear cotton.

America's healthful atmosphere like Los Angeles is unparalleled; India's spiritual atmosphere is superb. You only are missing here. I am constantly surrounded by a band of men and boys extremely devoted who are following me everywhere, joining me in deep contemplation [long hours of chanting and meditation] and plunging into any spiritual activity I want them to perform, asking no compensation. I have a chance to create from among them some good workers for spreading the cause. Here the men are as self-sacrificing as the ladies are in America. No words can express my happiness for your being the instrument of God in sending me here.

Internally, practically you have conquered the Divine Kingdom; and someday a time in your life would come when God would demand external renunciation from you, but not until you have fulfilled all of your duty to the cause. That's why the Lord didn't give you any children, that the cause may be your supreme child; and Mt. Washington is your supreme child, and its welfare and permanency you are ensuring of your own accord—with pleasure as you would do for your own child, and not with the consciousness of a burden. So am I happily doing for the work, my child.

I care not how I live, as I have renounced all for the cause. My tendency may be to tell you to live for the cause only. But please never be annoyed with me for suggesting to you what is best for the cause. I am happy for all you have done already, and will be glad to see you do whatever you can do; but never do I demand, neither do I ever feel sensitive if you reject any of my suggestions because of your circumstances. You are the only one in the world with whom I think aloud; and thus I feel happy and free with you to venture suggestions for the work, even though I know you have done for the cause as nobody else on earth has done.

It is very late, dear friend, 3 a.m. I am sitting within the mosquito curtain with an electric lamp, writing to you, enclosing my utmost love to you. Wherever God shall blow me, thither I shall go like the windblown leaf. Most of my work is done; I am happy. May you find fulfillment, utter victory over yourself, and be ever immersed in the bliss of God, in meditation and during the performance of the difficult duties which are required of you. People are flocking by the thousands. God is in the air; and the same God in me loves you forever.

Ever sincerely, supremely, I am yours.

* * * * *

Calcutta, India
December 6, 1935

Thank you for your three dear letters which were waiting for me when I came after a month's glorious time in Mysore. My life, you will notice throughout, is a constant big fight between Satan and God. But I rejoice that I always win in the end....

You will always notice, too, I never take the initiative in fighting until I am thrown in the arena by God. Dear one, if I were as a mendicant under a tree I wouldn't care whether people called me a Satan or a Christ. The only weakness of organization work is that I have to respond whenever I am attacked in order to keep respect of those who demand my spiritual service. Someday I will shed everything and be free. Mentally I am absolutely far away from the attacking vibrations of criticisms or praise; but physically I have to keep replying when criticized, for the sake of the students....Though Satan sometimes stops me in the beginning, God always makes Satan my footstool in the end. I can fully understand why Jesus for doing good got himself crucified by Judas. Modern Judases want to destroy not only the body but the soul and reputation. Praise or blame doesn't make me better

A GREAT YOGI OF THE EAST AND A GREAT YOGI OF THE WEST—MASTERS OF THEMSELVES

Paramahansa Yogananda and James J. Lynn in yoga posture on the private grounds of SRF Hermitage, Encinitas, California, 1950. "The balanced life of Mr. Lynn may serve as an inspiration for all men," the great Guru said. Conscientiously discharging the duties of his worldly life, Mr. Lynn yet found time daily for deep meditation on God. The successful businessman became an illumined *Kriya Yogi.*

or less, respectively; but a good reputation earned through the fire of criticism gives one the opportunity to do good. However, the power of evil goes with the wind, whereas the power of good goes against the wind.

My heart breaks to know of the immense responsibilities thrown on you....You and I are in the same boat, and we must weather stormiest trials together until we reach His shores.

I am pleased that you like my letters to you; that you are progressing on and on. Often I see your face gleaming with spiritual aureole and your light commingled with God. I feel you often in the Infinite Sea. Remember, as you approach nearer to God Satan gives up his mask and openly attacks the fleeing saint lest he forever escape into the eternal protection of God. But remember, virtue may be assailed but never hurt. When a child stabs a man with a knife, he spanks the boy but never feels like killing him. So it is with me; I must fight Satan, but I am neutral inside. He takes form and works through men to prevent the great work of a real devotee of God. So you are suffering from financial strain; yet you are expected to do your utmost for God, and for doing good and giving kindness, suffering this ordeal. Therefore rejoice; those that can do good under trying circumstances, blessed are they who suffer for His Name's sake and Guru's name's sake. What good karma you are storing in your bank of Eternity will never be exhausted. There are many rich men with idle money who do no good; you are fortunate and yet get hemmed in with financial strain. It was consciously taken away to test you that you might feel more for God's cause in spite of many trials. I have had to go through similar experiences; and the more I fight for righteousness, calmly and resigned to Him in utmost poverty, the more I find myself nearer to Him. He sent you to me when I was denied help from all humans; and God sent me to you in your torments and trials. You are using Divine Mother's money—every bit She has given to you belongs to Her—and She is highly pleased with you that you are spending for Her cause even under severe strain. She will never leave you out. When all will seem dark and still you go on doing and working for Her, She will Herself come to your rescue. So never feel sad when the strain is strong and severe on you. I walk on the Sea, burning behind me my boat of desire; and I know I won't be drowned.

God is deepening the well of your *samadhi.* It is a bottomless well of joy throughout eternity. Even when you will reach Finality, you will keep diving deeper into the ever new joy of the Well of Eternity. If God were finite Joy, then the souls—Jesus, Buddha, Lahiri Mahasaya, etc.—would get tired of Him and want diversion, and would want to come back on earth. But God is Eternal Joy, ever new Joy. He can endlessly entertain the saints with new Joy, ever-changing new Joy. The saints are so busy enjoying the Joy of Eternity afresh every day that they don't want any diversion of coming back to behold a new show in the earthly movie house.

My eternal unending love to you, the ideal of my soul of many lives.

I remain very sincerely yours.

P.S. Please write. Your letters are a great inspiration.

P.P.S. Ranchi is a great institution. I am so glad you like my action of acquiring it; it would be a mecca for Western and Eastern pilgrims of Yogoda. Congratulations are pouring in. Only thing Ranchi misses is your holy presence. Your spirit is hovering there and written in every blade of grass. Million thanks for saving Ranchi, which is my dearest child of nineteen years.

* * * * *

Calcutta, India
December 24, 1935

Greetings of Christmas and blessings of the New Year. May the Christ Consciousness remain enthroned in you forever and forever.

As Christ conquered Satan, so it has been my part to fight that force throughout my life. The nearer one approaches to God, the more consciously and tangibly Satan thwarts and annoys that devotee of God. ...One who is in league with Satan becomes a satan...carrying out the wishes of the Evil One....But we are in the army of God and the Gurus, and together we must fight it out. What an angel you have been; I wish I could tell you that.

I am happy beyond dreams that your meditation is deepening. I am happy beyond words that you are glad because of Ranchi. It is one of the greatest accomplishments in India, this year and for all times.

Days, nights, weeks, months, are passing; and with each footstep we are approaching our Eternal Kingdom. While millions are thinking they are approaching old age, death, and oblivion, we know we are approaching eternal life, eternal youth, eternal wisdom, eternal protection. So must you realize each day you are approaching Heaven. While you sit in meditation, expand your body, feeling the universe-body; the stars are the cells of your cosmic body. In mind, feel at once the minds of all. Standing amidst crowds, feel the limb and brain activity of all.

Stillness is the altar of Spirit. There is no limit of the deepening of stillness. There is no limit of ever new Joy. Never give mental boundaries to your perception of Joy. One thing pleases me most, that you feel deepening of Joy ever since you wrote to me: "My joy and bliss are growing deeper." That is what my beloved, blessed one always writes me, and what pleases me most. So no boundaries to your perception in meditation. No depths to be reached; you must keep expanding in universal consciousness and keep deepening your apperception of ever new unending Bliss. He is the inexhaustible Bliss who will entertain us throughout eternity, without cessation.

With love—ever my own boundless blessings to you.

P.S. Am seeing worthwhile saints; will tell you all about them.

*   *   *   *   *

Written from Ranchi, India
January 5, 1936

The busiest time of my stay here is growing, so I was compelled not to write to you last week. This is the first time I am writing to you from our most beautiful headquarters at Ranchi. Really this is very, very beautiful—the land of my ancient dreams, every inch of which ground is tinged with my life's blood and yearning to make a permanent temple in memory of Lahiri Mahasaya. No one in the whole world has given such great techniques [as the *Kriya Yoga* art and science], and my desire was to immortalize his name; and you have done it. This place is named Yogoda Satsanga/Self-Realization Fellowship, and Lahiri Mahasaya Mission, Ranchi. For the first time I have stayed here quite a few days, and I am loath to move anywhere else. Peaceful shades, innumerable fruit trees—mangoes, guava, papayas, litchi nuts (which you loved) like raisins when dried. There are wonderful jackfruit trees, huge fruits with yellow pulps and seeds; very nutritious. Your pleasure is mine, and some day when you see this property and meditate in its spacious shades, you will know how blest you are that you have helped immortalize this place. All Ranchi and India are blessing you. But for you and a few, it is becoming more and more difficult for me even in thought to get away from this spiritual environment.

I met a great yogi near Madras, Yogi Ramiah. Cobras, wild angry cobras, sleep on his hand whenever he touches them. He loves me very greatly. He and I entered into *samadhi* together. Very few are like him, when I compare him with ordinary creed-bound yogis and swamis.

I was detained in Mysore longer than expected, so my program is rather hurried. I am organizing a correspondence course here, exactly like ours [*Praecepta, Self-Realization Fellowship Lessons*], and arranging for its advertisement. I already advertised the school and many students have applied. I have been [economically] "frying the fish in the oil of the fish," specially that you be pleased to know how much good work has been already accomplished. I carried out a publicity campaign for the headquarters during a great *Kshatriya* conference (warrior prince's conference). About fourteen hundred princes gathered; our boys showed wonderful yoga feats of will power and strength; we had a rousing reception.

A papaya tree laden with fruits and saturated with God stands in front of my window as I am writing to you. Dear one, I have to finish a million things before I start; and I have to start soon, as I find the return permit to enter U.S.A. ends April 30, and I must lecture in London if possible. It looks like I have to start for U.S.A. by middle of February or 1st of March.

I am getting all data to write the life of Lahiri Mahasaya, which is so much needed in America and India. Dick is working hard setting up the correspondence course of *Praecepta Lessons* like that in America. He sends you his New Year's greetings along with mine.

Last night I was in *samadhi*. My pulse, my heart, stopped; my body was dead and my life force like a comet sprang through the spinal tunnel and head into the blue heavens. All matter became my dead within it I saw the Light of all life. I have been doing a million things; and I compared my divine state with work and I found this truth: Very few of us know how to differentiate between the duties created by us and the duties assigned to us by God. Most think of their own desire-created duties as divine duties. Human desire-created duties bind and cause reincarnation. Even those who know what divine duties are do not know how to accomplish them divinely, and instead picture and plan according to their own wishes. Self-created duties and ideas of performing them when frustrated cause great misery and disappointment; but divine duties performed divinely, whether frustrated or fulfilled, cause happiness in the doing—and in doing them again and again until God is pleased, whatever the results may be. Until we destroy our self-created pictures and hopes in doing even divine duties, we are slapped by delusion. Now I can say if all things are taken away I will never be sorry. I wanted the temple in Calcutta, but God frustrated it by a series of miraculous happenings and gave Ranchi, which satisfied me more than a million temples at Calcutta. Now I see I have always to find the Divine's wish, and also to perform it according to the Divine's wishes. Then there is infinite joy.

So must you remain immersed in your business ventures and do everything, all your duties, with ever-increasing ambition to perform them extremely well without ever caring if you meet resistance or temporary failure on your path. All we must do is repeatedly try to perform the divine duties until the inner satisfaction of making the super supreme effort is accomplished. First find what the divine duties are, then use your own ambition to accomplish them, asking God all the time to guide your creative effort and will to perform them as the Divine wishes.

Oh, such joy! I don't feel any sensations making any permanent impression in me. The ordinary man walks, sleeps, works, earns. I find I am settled in Bliss. I am awake in Bliss, ever watching the states of the body and mind when they are awake or asleep or dreaming. Last night I ate, and when I finished I didn't know I had eaten. All I knew was Bliss Eternal and Light ever spreading. Even now *Aum* is bounding over my head, tying it with the starry firmament. It is all very strange, all very secret. By meditation He makes the servant sit on the throne. Oh, this secret kingdom is yours and mine, beloved one. There is our permanent ashram, an astral hermitage, a bliss cavern, a celestial retreat of Eternity where we will dwell, ever entertained in ever new Bliss. With millions of blessings, billions of benedictions, and eternal love to you.

Ever yours sincerely.

*   *   *   *   *

[*Paramahansaji writes about the "Correspondence Course," the mailing from Ranchi of the printed* Yogoda Lessons, *which he prepared with the assistance of Dick Wright when they were in India.*]

See what you, beloved of all here, have started. This is first of its kind started in India, and is hailed as a great aid in spiritual reformation and clearing away the cloud of vagueness and mystical uncertainties from practical yoga and theology.

With love.

*   *   *   *   *

Written from Agra where Taj Mahal is.
January 30, 1936

Amidst splendor and grandeur in travels one face is missing; it is yours. Yet your soul is ever haunting every good scene, every saint we see, bringing you with us; and we say, "If he were only here." Such is life, and we do feel very very sad at times because your body is not here.

We saw two great saints in the *Kumbha Mela*. One was Uriya Swami. He was immersed in God. He has cured many lepers by divine grace. Utterly unassuming. I saw him privately and asked, "Give me a personal message." He replied, "You don't need one. Follow the path you are following." I asked, "Do you heal lepers?" He replied, "God does." He continued, "Why are you asking me about healing, for you do the same." We parted after communion. He asked me to speak to the vast concourse around him. The other, a young man, his eyes gleaming with God and wisdom, very learned. He has one piece of cloth, roams about by the Ganges, eating once daily whatever food is offered, sleeps in winter and summer without a blanket. It was shivering cold, yet his body was only half covered with one piece of thin cloth. Such life I wanted to live, but all the great ones I met told me that could not be; I had to teach and give my life for all. But now nothing matters, I am roaming in the forest of desirelessness anyway, even if I am not allowed to roam exclusively amidst the jungles of Himalayas.

Matters are becoming very difficult in my mind—the haunting melody of the spiritual life in India and the grand civilization of struggle in America. Were you with me, and a few of Mt. Washington, I would roam by the Jamuna, where Krishna played his flute of Eternity, and sing to Spirit and never visit the shores of material life. This I mean from my heart. America, I love her many things I wish were here; but I dread the financial struggle and the rigor and competition in getting financial support for religious work. It is you only who have made it possible for me to work with inspiration in writing, etc. In America, more money and prosperity, more attention and honor from people—renunciation, plain living are ignored—more material merging, more criticism. Here more God, more encouragement. I am between two boats. India has made fresh immortal marks in my soul, and I have an indelible love for America.

Yesterday we visited Dayalbagh near Agra, an ideal model city founded by a religious order, something which I always conceived of starting. Now my desire is fulfilled seeing this.

We saw the grandest monument erected to honor queen Mumtaz Mahal, the marble dream Taj Mahal. We saw the tomb of our greatest emperor Akbar. We dreadfully missed you amongst these scenes. Specially I missed you during *Kumbha Mela* at Allahabad, where you would have enjoyed meeting different saints, different lovers of God. I enjoyed these most during my stay here, and I know you would have enjoyed.

I told you Master has elected me as deputy president of his estate and Sadhu Sabha, and has blessed me by calling me Paramahansa.

I have found Him. I seek nothing; I wish nothing. Though I struggle, and plan, and work ambitiously, I am only doing His will. And you, my beloved one of all, who will see God through me, you are my second self, redeemer from my last responsibility to organized work. I am free. I am happy. Your spirit I shall take encased in my soul to God. Now the auto is waiting to go to Brindaban (Jerusalem of India where Krishna reigned) and to Delhi....

I find life is wonderful with God. It is an ocean of misery without

Him. Do your duty with utmost plan, but never be grieved if the desired result does not follow. Rather be grieved if your mind gets disturbed looking for results. Day and night I am planning, working for the cause as a man would plan for his home; but I have no desire. I am doing everything with the will of God and greatest freedom. Behold and feel the world wrapped with God; you will see gradually you do nothing because of *your* desire but because God wants you to do that. That is the real Paramahansa state. When you feel joy within after meditation, carry it all the time; don't ever lose it. Invest that joy in the bank of watchfulness and deep meditation. Then that joy will increase infinitely, and you will be a Croesus of joy. Then this joy you must give to the flowers, the blades of grass, men and women; cheer up the sad clouds and make the moon brighter and the sun more dazzling. Everything around you would consciously receive your joy and give you joy. Then you will know what you have acquired inside. You brought that joy into circulation. What is yours you must invest, until the joy of all will become your joy. Thank you a million times for fulfilling your part and helping me to carry on our work.

With deepest unending love, I am ever yours.

* * * * *

Written from Ranchi
February 21, 1936

I sent my re-entry permit back to Washington for time extension of six months. This was necessary to be done for completion of all work started here. The re-entry permit will be received by me during March and I will start in June. I hear there is a World Fellowship of Faiths Parliament of Religions in July in London. I expect to speak there and hold a lecture campaign and return to U.S.A. I am so happy you encourage and have redeemed the Los Angeles Mt. Washington Center. Our maharajas here start big things, but forget to found them on a permanent basis. I am so happy you are creating something lasting amidst fleeting time and fickle life....

I met a very great lady saint, Ananda Moyi Ma. She remains in *samadhi* most of the time. She is sweet and lovely beyond words, the highest conception of womanhood and representation of Divine

Mother. Her very presence is inspiring. She sat in communion with me for a long time. How wonderful it would be for the women of America if she ever goes there. She told me, "If you take me and ask Divine Mother, I will go." I will tell you more about her later.

I saw a vision in Bareilly, my home thirty years ago. There under the *sheoli* tree the flowers would fall on the altar of the dew-bedecked grass, and there I mingled my tears with the dew and worshipped God as He appeared to me as Light, gently blazing over the tender tips of the grassy altar. In my second visit recently, the *sheoli* tree was gone; but the light of God was still there, streaming and vaporizing tears of welcome as I entered. The old field where I played football, and ran and won many races, was there; the jasmine vine beneath which I smelled the aroma of God, was there too; the house, the field, the rooms, were all there, recognizable, neglected; but the dear human actors were gone. Such is the world. Before, thirty years ago, the neighbors and everybody knew me; now after thirty years, none knew me except by name or fame. Only our old school servant recognized me. Gone were the teachers, the little student friends, the romantic scenes of ancient past. I was moving amidst new actors and players. Then I asked God why all this; I thought it didn't pay to live too long to see so many loved ones go sailing by—never, perhaps, to return to ordinary human gaze. I was mortified when suddenly the scene became alive with memory and God. I saw everyone, every thing, just as they were before—my dead relatives and dead friends loomed up and spectre-like walked in broad daylight. What a stupendous scene! God can show us all we miss from the past, and also yet-to-be films not yet shown in the movie house of life.

So many dear ones slipped away since I last came here. Now I live no longer in delusive reality, but in a terrific dream. Realize this; live in Eternity. Don't live in the intoxication of the "now"; it is a terrible delusion. I see all the changes that are to be, and I am no longer interested in the present. So I tell you of the Divine's commandments. Very few follow the Divine's commandments, and very few have the fortune to hear about them—so many work fruitlessly and aimlessly. So remember, dear dear one, I speak not for my desires but for the desires of the Most High. He keeps me busy and expects me to do more and more, even when I think I have reached the limit of my capacity. This way He is building infinite capacity for work in me. He says, "Even as I bear the

burden of universes and meet all their demands, so must you grow lim-
itlessly patient, joyfully, continuously working for Me until you become
an eternal bold Doer like Me." So, beloved, bear with me. Look beyond; your kingdom and wealth is imperishable—it will never dimin-
ish. But of earthly things, give for God and God's work that you may be
declared a completely holy child of God, a modern Buddha of this age.
This is the glory I want you to attain by immortalizing Lahiri Mahasaya's
work and life-giving *Kriya Yoga* technique here and everywhere.

All my love to you. Yours forever, boundless love.

* * * * *

Written from Ranchi
March 17, 1936

In spite of all wisdom and perception, I feel very lonely since our
Guruji Swami Sri Yukteswar Giriji left us. Now you know, beloved one,
what consolation you have given me, what gratefulness you have won
from me and Guruji for being the divine instrument of making it possible for me to come here and pay to him my last respects on earth. I
wrote you, "Guruji is planning to give up his body. Perhaps I can stay
him." I had it all planned to go on March 6 to Puri where he was residing, but God didn't let me lest I pray to keep him here. Instead, I
started to go on March 8, and I was prevented. Then I went on March
9 and arrived at Puri March 10 morning, only to see his lifeless body
in *samadhi* posture. According to custom I had to bury his body in the
ashram grounds. The body which had reflected omnipresent wisdom
lay lifeless before me mocking, "I didn't let you pray for me."

On March 9, 7 p.m., our Guruji left his body; and about that time
he intimated to me of his departure. Also on the train I saw two tunnels of light and his astral self telling me of his departure. Though since
his departure I have been seeing him all of the time, practically, still it
is a great, great shock that I won't ever be able to show you and Mt.
Washington devotees Swami Sri Yukteswarji in body. He had told me,
"If I live through March (Bengali Chaitra month), I will live longer."
When I had asked him to see an American lady from California, he
replied, "I won't see her now, nor anyone else in this life." I know there
would have been a great battle if I was present at the time of his pass-

ing. I wrote a letter to him asking him not to give up his body, but the people through whom I sent it did not read it to him. Guruji was slightly feverish for five days. His fever left in the end; and while his body seemed perfectly well, he left in *samadhi*.

If there were words, I would write to you how I feel about the material disappearance of Master. Imagine, the Lord God did not want me to pray lest He have to grant my prayer or deny it. The lion has left his cage, the lion whose roar of wisdom kept me undergoing a thousand privations and demands of organization work. If I could weep, I would feel relieved. If I would cry, the gods would cry with me. If I had a thousand mouths, I would say India lost one of the greatest in wisdom. But the saddest of all is I could not show him you. But as Lahiri Mahasaya and I have taken you in our charge, you will meet them all in meditation and in Heaven, and just at the period of your transition from the body to immortality. But you are needed now, and the time is short and we must accomplish the task given unto us. Now that Guru is gone, you and I, comrade dear, have to shoulder the work. Bear with me all. It's unbearable; he is gone. No more all shall see him; only the few who can reach him. Once the lips are sealed, saints and savants must keep quiet until such time through another body the voice speaks. Henceforth, my Master shall speak through me. Though he is gone forever for earthly people, he is divinely haunting me day and night. I see him in every direction I turn my eyes. Oh, what paradox, he shall speak with me but with few else; such is the decree.

The answer to my going away to roam by the Ganges and in the Himalayas is grievously answered by my Master. Another bondage of work and responsibility thrown on me. In the terrible heat I am working day and night to straighten matters. Beloved, bear with me; you and I are in the same boat. Your life and soul the Masters have consecrated; fear not.

Yours in the immortal kingdom. Receive my love; I am with you always. A million times, love and blessings.

Very sincerely yours.

P.S. It is your sight and company again that will lessen somewhat of what I have lost in earth life. Please do write to me. Ever my love and eternal benediction. Very sincerely yours.

Herewith enclosed a picture of Master in final *samadhi* in garland.

* * * * *

Calcutta, India
April 6, 1936

Your most expected missive dated February 29 at last reached me. You must have received my cablegram via Los Angeles announcing the passing of our lord [Swami Sri Yukteswar] on March 9. If I could cry I would feel relieved. I am sorry for all. Eternity has sealed his lips to most human ears. I am sad, even though I see him at every turn of my gaze. He was one of the wisest men, greater in exposition of wisdom than Shankara as far as I know. When comes such another? I am remembering all the divine play and communion he had with me. I can hardly think anything else these days than of all his untold gifts of upliftment given to me. I saw many teachers, but none like our lord who was a spiritual lion, never bending, ever aflame with wisdom. Your expression of desire to come here all the more pained me now that the main incentive of your coming is gone.

We are puppets dancing with strings of emotions and habits on the stage of time, unless we redeem ourselves from the wheels of karma by reclaiming our lost divinity. I never saw the futility of worldly life as now. I am between two fires: my thoughts of you, principally, and our charge at Mt. Washington and the dear students there and in U.S.A., and on the other side the caves of the Himalayas and the banks of the Ganges where roam many free people of God. A thousand memories of Master's uncompromising freedom are haunting me. And I to lose that freedom going to the U.S.A. again? And to think of the dilemma of financing the organization, which you are so kindly doing. I have to think what is best. Even now as I am writing I can see Master in front of my eyes smiling at me, calling me from all sides: "Yea, I am free. Behold my freedom and uninterrupted roaming in the land of Eternity. Yea, you are yet a prisoner of duties." I wonder if the mighty wind would sweep away all my spiritual karmic duties and let me go free in the woodlands of India.

Dear one, I am deeply grateful that you are thinking of providing funds for the real ones. Why wait; let it start now. Please order Mt.

Washington to put half of what you give in a trust fund, let C. C. [correspondence course, *Self-Realization Fellowship Lessons*] be managed by half of what you give. This must be done before I return. Though C. C. has not paid yet, it has immortalized the *Lessons,* which I would not have written without the proper incentive. Even in the circle of saints, I hear highest praises about the *Lessons,* for systematizing the steps of realization so scattered and buried in yoga books. An immortal work has been done. Besides, all our members, and specially real seekers, who cannot come in touch with me personally (which is impossible to do; life is too short and distances too great) unanimously agree how well pleased they are with the *Lessons.* Even if we advertise less, we must not give up the *Lessons.* About criticism, there will be always some sort or other. What people receive free they don't appreciate, and the good seekers would appreciate even if they have to pay, just judging from the instructive value of the *Lessons* and the benefit they derive therefrom....I know from my experience in Europe and India that my *Lessons* are visible proof of the spreading of Lahiri Mahasaya's teachings. Lectures evaporate from the minds of the many (except real seekers, whose percentage is very little), but written lessons stand as permanent proof of the depths and practicality of a teaching. We should never abandon the system of *Lessons;* that's the only way of keeping our people steadily going on in this path. Also the magazine, though not paying, has done immortal work in India and the world. I have heard great comments. Advertising brings curiosity seekers in abundance who support the work temporarily, but it also brings real seekers gradually, who would never know of our teachings otherwise. How could people in South America, London, Australia, New Zealand, India, be benefitted by our teachings unless they receive through C. C.? I have no time and would not waste time as a travelling lecturer. Those that are thirsty would come to me or drink from my written teachings impregnated from my soul's perception. I want to serve by keeping myself constantly recharged with God....

You will be pleased to know that I have been working incessantly for creating a permanent center in Calcutta, the crown city of Bengal, and I think I am almost successful....Ranchi is rapidly progressing. I sent you the school prospectus, which I hope you received. You have done so much to manifest my wishes and have found consolation and divine satisfaction. Think how gracious and wise it was for you to let me come when Master astrally intimated to me of his passing. He actually extended his visit on this globe for sixteen years and waited for my coming. He would not have waited longer.

Now I humbly request you by the same divine command not to give Satan opportunity to cause us and our work trouble, but to start a trust fund for the real seekers at Mt. Washington, even in a small way right from now on. This will make me very happy, and I will not mind to go through any personal trouble or risk or living on husks if I felt Mt. Washington was becoming secure. You are the chosen instrument of God; you can do it, you must, none else can, for you are the chosen one. That is your spiritual test and supreme problem to solve. God has given you no child for that reason, that you may provide and make secure your spiritual child of Mt. Washington. This would remove from us the desire to make C. C. paying. C. C. would be used as a divine agent only to uplift people and not be thought as a means of financial support, even to make the work self-supporting.

Never have I realized more than now that the one purpose of all life is to seek God until one finds Him. So all our powers must be used to find Him, and then our God-intoxicated example will serve to redeem others. There is only one way to uplift people, that is to meditate all the time and be so saturated with God that whoever comes in contact will know and feel that divine Presence. Be in God and let sincere seekers be invited by your magnetism to watch you merged in God. That is the best silent way of lecturing and converting people. Think God, enjoy God, live God, love God, dream God, do all things for God. Walk, talk, think, work, move, carry on business for God alone. Enjoy God and let others enjoy Him through your living example. God can be given through words, a look, touch, writings only by those who have touched God. God has created this nightmare of earthly existence—rather this scant dream of life mixed with nightmares—that some day we will be disgusted of it and try to wake up and enjoy His immortal joy.

Ever my heart gives you all I have. I am storing Self-realization for you, which you shall have added to your own—what you have acquired and are acquiring on earth. When you leave for the Eternal Kingdom, that will be your permanent provision in Heaven.

With deepest love, ever yours.

Calcutta
April 27, 1936

Your big typewritten letter and also a handwritten letter were gladly received. I was overjoyed to know that at last you sanctified and gladdened the hermitage at Mt. Washington by your presence. I really am very pleased, and that you have a clear perspective of things and have candidly estimated and appreciated the nature of the residents there. It took me years to put down disorder, and really I succeeded when I started with young people. It took a great deal of time, effort, and patience to smooth the moods, stubbornness, and habits of residents there. I had to bear the brunt, and I fully appreciate when you have found out the mettle of the true ones.

I want to tell you my opinion about what I see: About commercializing our work, I really do hate to see anyone commercializing religion. By commercializing it means "using religion for individual benefit or benefit of the business." Are we doing that? No. Then what are we doing? We are not using religion for business, but we are using business methods in religion, which we must do. Sincere seekers won't be found in a hundred years unless they know me and our work. The quicker they know through advertisements, the better it is. Some may turn away because of advertisements, but careful wording would not turn sincere seekers away; they would be increasingly found....Aren't Bibles sold? Somebody has to pay for them. What sin in selling to-the-point benefitting instructions and using the money to print more of such. You must know of hundreds of others who hungrily wait for the weekly *Lessons*. Sincere seekers are satisfied with truth, and they never mind helping the cause of spreading same by paying....

Master's passing has left me desolate in the world, though not in the Spirit world. I would cry with a thousand eyes if I could, but I can't. How sad I feel; for what the world has missed, it will never know. We are in this world for a little while to play our parts, and then we are drawn away suddenly and all our responsibilities and self-created magnified cares have to cease. The Lord is the doer. We must do all we can to see Him within and in all our work; that is the truth for which all human beings should live and act and think and will and work. India with all her deficiencies is full of that consciousness of God in everything. I sleep little at night. Tunnels of life envelop me; they burst

Mr. Lynn in meditation at the Mother Center, 1937. The disciple's slight smile conveys an intimation of the bliss that he habitually enjoyed in God-communion. "A master is not a master of someone else, but of himself," he said. "Even God does not try to master others. He has given us life, consciousness, and free will to live the divine life if we choose."

across infinity showing me the place where you and I and all must go, where I see Master roaming.

I have so far booked passage for two in the *Kaiser-I-Hind;* one is pending. Let us see what God wants, for I only want to do His will and nothing more. Our car has to be turned over to the customs after one year ending July 11, 1936, otherwise they would charge us heavy duty. This is one reason for starting so early, and the other one you know—I want to see you soon, God willing.

With boundless love and blessings, I am very sincerely yours.

*   *   *   *   *

Srinagar, Kashmir, India
May 19, 1936

Your very delightful cablegram expressed your welcome from your heart. It is wonderful to feel your welcoming love. That is the grandest reason that I am going now, overcoming my greatest temptation to do away with all material connection with organization and walk and roam by the Ganges in Hardwar with the Infinite. First I must inform you that I am starting for England by *S. S. Chitral* starting June 13. I couldn't make Kashmir and go by 23rd of May (*Kaiser-I-Hind* steamer). My body has to pass through certain changes due to taking of other's karma all the time, and lots of impediments coming my way. But I guess everything will be all right in the end.

My heart died within me not to have you with us here in this beautiful vale of Kashmir with lakes—Dal Lake and houseboat (in which this short letter is being written). The car is waiting to leave for Lahore, thence to Bombay for lecture, thence to Calcutta and back again to start for England, God willing. Ettie and Dick have left Calcutta for good. Will remain in Bombay until I join them. Many things remain unfinished here due to the advent of summer weather (wholly unfit for lectures). I would have to wait for one year and winter to finish all things. But a great many things were accomplished by you and me: Ranchi established, Calcutta center on the way to permanency, Bangalore center established, all India publicity very favorably carried, C. C. [*Yogoda Lessons*] established and wonderful workers secured, and many other things accomplished. Our work is known all over India and its furtherance would be easier. However, beloved one, know this for certain: for you principally I am going back to America to settle all things until I have my final freedom from everything; for the freer I am the more I can give freely.

Here is a temple of Shankara on a mountain top, which transformed into Mt. Washington Center when I first beheld it nineteen years ago with Guruji. He is gone, but he is more with me, altared in the sunshine, the water, on the boat, and in the trees circling the bank.

You have served as one of the greatest instruments to bring East and West together, and I have made a place for you in Heaven where you will sit by me and Lahiri Mahasaya. Ever be diving deep and deeper, unto eternity, never seeking the end, for ever new bliss is eternal.

With deepest love to you and the group. I loved to hear of your visit and encouragement and spiritual upliftment of Mt. Washington; everybody was overjoyed.

With eternal love.

Ever yours.

*   *   *   *   *

Bombay, India
June 17, 1936

You must be thinking it strange why I do not come after so much fuss. Well, it was providential as well as the fault of the steamship company. In the last minute they refused space for the car; besides, just the day before sailing came extremely important things. One of them is that I had left Master's estate half finished. Really I should never have agreed to go without making things definite....By a miracle alone we got the deeds out and the Puri property is ours. The buildings need repair and we must sometime put up a temple over where Master is buried in the sitting *samadhi* posture. I have placed Swami Sevananda in charge.

Blessed one, you know not what work you have started in Ranchi. ...This institution has sailed through uncertain seas for nineteen years. Now I have through your instrumentality incorporated it and given it to [be governed by] a board of directors; it could never become private property or even returned to me.

Already I bought a few cows and our milk has increased from 30 lbs. to 60, and now the thin little boys are getting more robust. I have opened a scientific gymnasium with apparatus and Yogoda exercises, which has greatly roused public interest. And I have a wonderful athlete in charge. Day and night for months I have spent in sultry Calcutta to fix all these things....

It was Master who commanded me to create a school of yoga discipline (high school plus yoga training); and think, it was you, the noble instrument that was awaited to lay its foundation—and now please make it permanent and doubly earn the immortal gratefulness of needy India.

I often see Master and he blesses you; and Lahiri Mahasaya loves you—you are dearly and kindly watched by him. I have told you this, breaking the laws of divine secrecy.

I wish you could see the boys here who are most self-sacrificing and religious. So many remain awake meditating all night with me.

I'm happy you went and inspired and resurrected the spirit of the divine ones at Mt. Washington. Really, I waited ten years to find the ones that are in Mt. Washington, whose merit I am so happy you have come to recognize. They all are truly your own people, and you all are really my people. Just being relatives doesn't necessarily or often make them your own. When we gather in the name of God, justice, and right action, then we build a family of heaven, and there is much happiness there.

In front of my hotel here in Bombay, under the roof of the building across from me, night before yesterday, appeared a great light and then a figure. After looking very scrutinizingly (for I thought it was a cloud) I saw Lord Krishna standing and playing his flute. He smiled and waved at me, and gradually vanished in the sky. I thought, what did I do to deserve all this?

Night passes in untold joy, and day in the thrill of doing and working for the Lord and Guru. Haven't we thrilled every moment in the path of divine living. Such is God, so good to His devotees. He keeps them drunk with the wine of everlasting bliss. What a companion God has given me that you understand me and my actions as They [God and Guru] divinely guided. I had not to convince you why I wanted to come to India, except I had to tell you that my Master wanted to go from this earth; and you were so understanding. Oh, how can I thank you for listening to me, for being so sympathetic, sacrificing, and understanding. Indeed in a millennium, once in a while one gets a genuine friend in everything, like you.

I have made a mansion of light for thee in Heaven; and therein you and I will dwell with just a few others before we merge in the Infinite. We shall be able to materialize and be in our earthly form in Heaven whenever we would want to do so. The glory of Heaven few know. It is definite to those to whom it is revealed. It is the kingdom of various lights, and garlands of lights, just behind matter, where the divine ones come out of the Infinite, or go back from the earth, to love and play with God in many forms of saints. This is very secret knowledge known to few. You and I will meet Lahiri Mahasaya first, then Babaji, then Guru Swami Sri Yukteswarji. This is a prophecy to your soul to be enacted when we will shed our mortal coil.

Behold when our bodies are gone; then why delusion even now? With all you have, like [the renunciation of] Buddha, help in creation of ashrams in India where God's children can dwell and meditate. Much is expected of you, for you belong to the extraordinary class of disciples. Many would be redeemed through you. I am so happy at last you realize why I wanted you to take up leadership or serviceship, a training in rejoicing with God in other souls. The humble ones receive the greatest benefit. Only after doing and performing the divine commandments which come through us can one realize that One who wholly guides us. We live only to please God. We wish nothing but day and night to seek ambitiously to do what God and the Great Ones wish. Any anxiety I show in any direction is because of the Divine's promptings. I am in tune with the Masters; the Masters are in tune with God; and you, being in tune with me, are in tune with the Masters and God. This is the way it works. Those who understand this secret never break this law, and uninterruptedly and easily reach the goal through the invisible leading hand of their Guru-Guide. Others doubt and fall in the ditch of spiritual inertia. Prepare yourself, day and night increasing the wealth of your joy, awakening souls in the light of your joy, and renouncing all for God. With all my love to you. Do go often to Mt. Washington.

With deepest love, ever yours.

Paramahansa Yogananda and Rajarsi Janakananda in SRF Hermitage garden, Encinitas, California, 1938

P.S. Do help me to work the Divine's wish here, and then I shall go happy. I feel I must accomplish definite things here after I stayed in America sixteen years. With love eternal, ever yours.

* * * * *

Bombay, India
June 26, 1936

It staggers one's imagination, and one is filled with the ecstasy of joy to recall the evening you walked like a child into the hall of my recognition in Kansas City. Think, ever since what heavenly friendship we have enjoyed. Think how our mutual celestial joy has multiplied. Think how much we have accomplished together to alleviate human suffering, and have brought so many to taste the spring of eternal happiness. Think what a combination you and I are. I had asked Divine Mother—I tell you actually, I prayed—for a saintly businessman who would act as a divine comrade to serve this work as his own work. Divine Mother consented, for you had been born for this purpose. How many times we have seen the Divine together in the temple of ecstasy. To think of all that has transpired between you and me is to open the spring of an unending joy—such joy, such mutual sincerity and happiness in doing God's work together. Dreams about our divine communion often flit by my mind, and I have caught one of those dreams of happiness and painted it in words as it comes straight from the chamber of my heart.

I have been detained here for a few days meeting some important people. Soon I will be going to Ranchi and Calcutta to finish the rest of the affairs in connection with Master's estate.

I have something sacred to tell you. I feel Master is everywhere, and I have within something immortal as to how he came to me on the 19th of June and showed me his resurrected body. I cried aloud, "Is it, my lord, the same body that was interred in the salt and soil at Puri?" And he said, "Yes, it is so; I am alive evermore. Tell this to Saint Lynn, tell everybody, I have come away from a real dream world and have appeared really in your dream world. I was real then; I am real now." Your name he uttered first. I have written in detail all that happened, and I will personally give that to you, if God be willing. All the questions that remained unanswered—that he hadn't answered—he answered them all. It was stupendous, baffling, touching, heart-thrilling. My Master was a very hard disciplinarian. He scolded everybody; he didn't spare me. Very few passed under his hard test. He told me, "I am sorry I scolded you so much. None passed my test as you, and I will scold you no more. You and I will never lose each other unto eternity; and unto eternity I will not scold you or wear a scolding on my face. I shall always smile with you." I cried, and I embraced him again and again: "Master, beloved mine, scold me; do scold me through eternity. I love to be scolded by you." In the vision I touched him, and I talked with him. I feel that immortal touch every day all over my body, that all-solacing touch. And then my Master went away.

If I had a thousand voices I would cry to the world about his resurrection in this new way. He is alive, ever watching the growth of our work and the homecoming of matter-tired, matter-stricken souls. Oh what tears, oh what joy! I wish you had been here with him; and think, he spoke your name first: "Tell Saint Lynn, this is my same body which you buried in the sands of Puri resurrected evermore." Think, he too called you saint. That standard is being kept by you; and which you will keep to eternity—an exemplary life for Americans and Hindus equally to follow.

It is up to us during the short span of our lives to do our best, our utmost, nothing sparing for the upliftment of souls in India and America. The physical and spiritual suffering of men bleeds my heart, especially of the suffering people of India, the most spiritual nation of the earth. India in her pristine glory was a land of the gods, now fallen and poverty-ridden, still trying to bring His ancient ideals into practice.

Forget not, dear one, that the weekly *Lessons* are the best means to awaken the people of the West; and that must be made known to most people of the world that we might comb out the sincere ones. I have worked many years in America. The sincere ones are few among many, and they remain with me; but the many would-be sincere ones need literature and study to ripen their sincerity. The best way to reach them is through notice of our work in magazines, etc. The trouble with myself going around, they want me and no lesser personality after I have once gone to a place. This way I have been indirectly the cause of ruining [slowing the growth of] my work in many places. But those who go through training through correspondence receive great inspiration and don't depend only on me. If they are very sincere, as Sister Gyana-mata who corresponded for years and then she came, they also would ultimately come to me. I cannot and will not waste my time in lectur-ing much, unless God inspires me to do so. My life's time I want to spend in writing, God-ecstasy, singing, dancing in *samadhi,* and teach-ing those who come to me, by the very life I live, how to contact God.

I wish you were present in our Students' Home in Calcutta where the ex-students of Ranchi Vidyalaya have clustered together. There on Saturday nights in the gatherings I have sung and danced [as did Sri Chaitanya and his disciples]; and at the end of the dance I have let my body go into rigid ecstasy. I feel I am swimming in the ecstasy while I dance, then all becomes light and my body falls lifeless to the ground. Sometimes I watch my lifeless form on the ground swimming in God; and sometimes I see the Ocean of Happiness in which the body is no more. Sing to yourself the song you like and you will get *bhakti* (devotion) *samadhi,* which God loves also from His devotees. As the women of America are very spiritual and given to loving God, so are the boys here. I have extremely enjoyed my ecstasies with them when all or most of the boys and men would become God-stricken with me on these occasions. The night before I came here, all night, I sang and danced—swam in the Infinite. Oh what joy, beloved mine! The joy you are enjoying is the same immortal waters from which you and I and all true devotees drink.

Life is not long; life's time is short. Vivekananda, Ramakrishna, and Sister Nivedita (Miss Margaret Noble, who has established a great girls' school at Calcutta and also helped Vivekananda to establish Belur Math by the Ganges) are names now, yet are living and working with the masses wonderfully by creating hospitals, dispensaries, schools. So also Lahiri Mahasaya, Sri Yukteswarji, are living names, and Saint Lynn and I would be living names, creating hermitages for God-contact everywhere....Spiritual forces work silently but surely with the souls of men. This has been the prophecy of this generation. Rouse yourself to the height, and uplift the names of India through me. Ranchi made per-manent and work spread out from there would be a spiritual beacon light to warm India with new happiness and save her from the chill of poverty and endless miseries. Now do let us plan together. I am ready to play my part with my life, my heart, my soul. We must build our work today in a way that makes it imperishable, so that if we depart today from the earth the work would go on....

I've had nineteen years of struggle and uncertainty. I have been patient long enough; and because you have brought the institution to such heights, I'd like to see that institution and its work completed. I want to do justice to what you have already done, that you may be pleased forever because of all I have done through your help.

Ever be close to the Lord through work (public-benefiting work) and meditation. These are the two horses to be fitted to the chariot which shall soar heavenward and carry you and those that believe in you to God. I have made a place for you there. Fear not. Forsake all for God; and I say unto you, you will gain the universe. All that you have done for God is treasured into the bank of Eternity for you for further work, wherever you go now and hereafter.

With deepest love to you. I am awfully happy you were the object of such inspiration to the divine people at Mt. Washington.

Ever yours.

*   *   *   *   *

Bombay, India
July 1, 1936

Oh, what joy it has been to work with you in developing the wishes of the Masters. Now that Guru is gone and has left me with his wishes, it is our joyous responsibility to work them out to our best. I have burnt my boats, and have launched myself into the ocean of divine work. And you, my fellow comrade, my own, are there to help me through the storms of difficulties. I have no ambitions for myself, not even a little for the work or for my own glory; but I am very very ambitious to satisfy the wishes of the Masters and to work the wishes of God. They overwhelmingly put their desires in my mind so that I can do utmost in this short span of life. I am always asked to do more; I am kept busy. That's why I write to you about so many projects. All you are required is to do your best for now. You are working not for a small family, or individual ambition of power and wealth, but that God's humble work may be carried on by souls like you who are loved of God and whose lives are consecrated to God....

Dear one, you have done more than anybody on earth; that's why not for myself but for God's work and Gurus' commandments and wishes I have so freely told you all I felt about the development of the work. Privately, great saints and Yogodans here know you are the secret Saint Lynn who without the love of name and fame has founded this work on a living foundation and saved it from untold difficulties. Blessed one, fill yourself with the courage and renunciation of Buddha; do your best for God the little while we are here in the cosmic cinema. Think how many have lived, now gone and forgotten, in the very land and acreage in which you are living; but your name will be immortal with God. Fearlessly follow me, courageously follow me and my divine inspirations. So far there has been much happiness, as you often yourself express; for you have gained God, and gained much happiness, for saving this work. As you shall follow to the end in utmost faith and act up to my inspirations, eternal joy is waiting for you; you shall gain more and more the everlasting treasure. Earthly treasure is perishable and shall perish, but it can do imperishable work. You are ordained to do that aspect, as I am ordained to do the spiritual aspect; and we have to do both the spiritual and material good whenever necessary.

My pen has not stopped. I hardly ever write to you before I feel God. He has been dictating to me all I have written. I have no responsibility in the matter. See this; behold this blazoning light of God behind the thoughts and words of my letters. Now the world is receding, and my pen is surrounded with a halo of light. Everything is ablaze, even the ink. I can hardly perceive what I am writing; only I know the Light is writing through me. Every letter, every word in this letter, carries the wishes of God and a message for you, my divine one.

We are expected to do much in the short span of our lives. The Divine usually recalls messengers of truth after their work is done. Think, because I was in America Master lived sixteen years longer. But now that I came, he left the responsibility on my shoulders and went. I am glad I saw him; and I am overjoyed that I saw his resurrection—about which I shall tell you when I see you.

As you see the sky, know it is the Lord looking at you. As you look at the sun, know that the Lord is giving vitality to you. As you look at the moon, know the Lord is giving you love. As you look at the flowers, know that the Lord is smiling at you. As you look at people, know the Lord is asking to be recognized and crying for deliverance. As you look at saints, know that the Lord is talking to you.

As I sit still, I become more still. Stillness has many screens, so has realization many layers. You must never think you have found the last stillness, last realization, or last joy. Whenever you feel you have reached the climax of stillness or realization or joy, seek further, and you will enter into a finer, deeper state. Go on doing that unto eternity, and still you will say God is inexhaustible. So are we seeking God that our perceptions may never grow stale and our growing hunger for joy may never get satiated or saturated throughout eternity. This is the way; follow eternally, going behind each deeper perception. Peel them like onions, and God will be ever hiding behind every layer of perception.

With eternal love to you. Ever yours.

* * * * *

Ranchi, India
July 12, 1936

For the first time I am writing to you on our Ranchi Ashrama stationery. The philomel is cooing, innumerable birds are singing, mangoes by the hundreds temptingly hanging from the trees, guavas, jackfruit, flowers, are all inviting you. If only your body were here; your spirit is here, for almost everybody knows you—you the instrument divine to help stabilize one of India's healthiest hilly *ashramas* where many devotees are growing in God. The fortnightly instructions have started off on July 1, the actual date when we promised to send out *Lessons.* We brought a fine mimeograph; and Dick came in very handy training two efficient workers for setting up the *Praecepta.* This was one of my great wishes fulfilled. Without a central teaching as foundation, no work can go on. We will immortalize the work in the *Praecepta.* Sometime you will realize what amount of work was done since I came here—all because of your loving help.

The Heavenly Father and the Great Ones want you and me to do utmost while we are in these bodies. You and I will only once be Lynn and Yogananda. So we must do our utmost now to do all Lynn and Yogananda are expected to do. If we remain in hopes of doing everything in future, interruptions will come and our work will remain un-finished....

The Divine, having infinite capacity for doing good in His own creation, expects His children, made in His own Image, to do more than they think they can do. Think, after a few years how many will walk and work in Kansas City and Los Angeles and India after Lynn and Yogananda are gone. We must work sufficiently, extensively, qualitatively, so that our names will have a magic spell and inspiration for all those who follow us, to be inspired to expand the work which we leave behind us....

We are a little while playing in this cosmic cinema. The box office is open; the house is full, and we are on the screen and have shown some of our work. The climax has to be reached, and then the audience will be thrilled with our everlasting picture. Then we will disappear during the intermission of earthly departure. But even though we would be gone, our work will be repeated; in the continuous film we will work for all time to come. Our combination is not fortuitous or by chance. We are ordained to be together, and that's why every moment of our lives must be first spent in meditating and then also planning for the redemption of others that they too might meditate upon God and find Him.

A mist of light spreads over the half portion of this letter where I have marked X, and I am writing in a light of blended sunlight and astral light. Blessed one, your name is written in Heaven by mine—we the two forces of Lahiri Mahasaya and Guru to work and immortalize their message here. The Great Ones are completing their karma (actions) by working through us, and we are completing our karma (actions) through the devoted ones at Mt. Washington and here.

Meditate and enjoy bliss eternally. With love eternal, ever yours.

* * * * *

Ranchi, India
July 19, 1936

This letter would be a hasty one as the mail is soon leaving. I have been regularly writing to you every week as the Divine actuates me. I know the matters are stupendous and difficult, but the Divine always wants us to know that we have all the powers necessary to work God's plans, provided we make up our mind and work very hard and continuously to accomplish them. I am inspired by your cooperation and divine instrumentality. Considering that the time of life is short (of which many years already have been spent), we have to accomplish much. That's why the Divine is pouring instructions through me....

Last night was Saturday meeting and singing. I fell into a trance. I saw my beloved Guruji. He moved and walked all about in front of me, consoling and blessing me. He asked me to remove the sandalwood mark on his forehead on his picture in the *ashrama.* Strange, he never liked [ritual] decorations like that while living; now that he is ever-living, he came and acted as before when he was living.

Great is my joy. I am planning, working, yet I am free, completely free even amidst my divine ambitions. Nothing can hurt me. Nothing can take away my joy, even if the whole world were taken away from me. Such joy—such joy that I feel the universe as my heart bursting with unending joy, ever new Bliss. Beloved one, press on incessantly until you conquer the universe. The kingdom of Bliss is spread tier upon tier unendingly, beyond the blue vaults of heaven. No matter how much joy you have, look for more and you will get it. Haven't your joys been ever increasing? That's why you are so fortunate. When joy is same, that is stagnation. We have to march on endlessly in the eternal ether of meditation.

A few days left before starting [on return journey] August 22, God willing. Will cable. I don't plan anything now except through the Divine.

Do your mightiest even as Buddha did. Little did you dream what you would be called upon to do; and the more you are doing the more your power to do divine work is increasing. Keep on, fear not; God will give you all the supply you need, provided you go through all the trials and tribulations of God's test for His name and work's sake. Our home and family is God and God's work, so we must work hard to maintain it, even as a family man does everything to support his family. Our life is dedicated on the altar of God. We must become His in every way.

With deepest love and blessings to you, my beloved one of many lives. Ever yours.

Mr. Lynn on a seagirt rock, Encinitas, 1936. "The love of God is the only Reality," he said. "We must realize this love of God—so great, so joyful, I could not even begin to tell you how great it is!"

Ranchi, India
August 6, 1936

I cannot express my joy to know how, Buddha-like, you are more and more internally and externally giving yourself for this work. I have given everything; so are you, a true comrade born out of my prayers: "Divine Mother, send my own unto me who would first be devoted unto Thee and me, and then materially to carry on this work, unselfishly without egoism or pride." When I think of it, that my prayers were consciously answered in you, I become overwhelmed with joy and tears trickle from my eyes. Think, the unmaterial became material, and you have become the chosen instrument of the Divine to be able to do such mighty work here and in America. Many wished for that role, but you were chosen. Think how the Divine is not only with you but constantly doing great work through you. All my demands through the Divine you have graciously answered; I am happy beyond dreams. It is wonderful to be able to do such teamwork. Two God's stallions, power divine and spirituality combined, together pulling the chariot of the Gurus' work, which will carry many souls out of the hades of horror and sorrow to the paradise of peace and freedom....

I am so happy you have grown to love Mt. Washington and appreciate those that I have trained with greatest painstaking care. My children at Mt. Washington are like children, and of such is the kingdom of God. I am very happy that you understand them and love to meditate with them. I daresay the ones that are in tune with me are divine and can be found in very few places in the world. They are those along with you whose seats are reserved in Heaven. I am so happy you've made a second visit. Please do come often, for it is your real home. I have sprinkled the invisible nectar of my spiritual attainment mostly at Mt. Washington and Ranchi....

Last of all, this morning I put one of the small boys, a companion of Swami Sri Yukteswarji, into trance; and I called Guruji, and he came. The boy consciously saw him, talked with him. Guruji was pleased to come, was smiling and blessed me, and told me he would come whenever called. The boy was filled with joy; and we were lost in happiness. Through all, Master was smiling. It was a real experience; it was most thrilling. A few who were with me in my room were translated with ecstasy.

There are two individual dissolutions or "floods." First the partial dissolution of sleep and second, the bigger dissolution of death. (1) The partial dissolution of sleep every day dissolves the daily picture of life; unconsciously, the soul realizes its invisible blessed nature. (2) Death is a bigger dissolution in which the soul first finds out that the body is only a shadow, a picture played on the screen of the cosmic cinema house. Both of those above processes are unconsciously imposed upon man. Therefore yogis learn to produce partial dissolution and the bigger dissolution consciously by *pranayama,* switching off the life force from the sensory and motor nerves (as in sleep), and further switching off the life force from the sensory and motor nerves, muscles, lungs, heart, spinal cord, seven plexuses, etc. In order to destroy the false reality of the body and its surroundings, and to behold this body and world as pictures, and to understand the invisibility and real nature of the soul, the yogi must be able to produce the partial dissolution— Sanskrit *khanda* (partial) *pralaya* (dissolution) and *mahapralaya* (bigger dissolution) at will. *Mahapralaya* is the way Master went.

Please practice these two states—of sensory-motor *samadhi* with heartbeat and sensory-motor relaxation *samadhi* without heartbeat—and you will know this universe as God's cosmic cinema house. Please realize this. I am living a little in this world for this work, but mostly I am creating partial and bigger dissolutions. So this universe is actually a picture show to me, and you and I are God's loved players.

We are all ready to leave on August 22. Oh, how I will love to see you, as if after another incarnation.

With deepest, deepest love to my beloved one. Many blessings and love to those at Mt. Washington. Ever yours in the service of the Lord God and Gurus.

* * * * *

Bombay, India
August 20, 1936

Your kindest cablegram arrived safely; Ranchi headquarters is now a firmly established institution....You have satisfied one of the great divine wishes in me and I am supremely pleased....I am leaving India with the greatest satisfaction, and the Lord shall give you greater satisfaction for fulfilling this nineteen years of dreams....

Your life has been a shooting star getting nearer and nearer to Heaven. Please keep that way; change no more. We shall race to Heaven together as soon as our work here becomes finished. But we have to do much yet for needy India. You have started a work here that will keep growing; and our names will work after our bodies are gone. Isn't that wonderful—that we shall work impersonally, bodilessly, even after we are gone. But that's later; we have now the pleasure to see our already growing work grow bigger....

Yesterday afternoon as I sat in a half-meditation state, Satan dropped onto my body and pulled my astral body out of my physical body; my heart stopped. Then Guru as an angel of God appeared and warned me, saying, "Look, look what Satan is doing unto thee!" I made an effort; and like a stretched rubberband my astral body slipped back into my lifeless frame, and I cried out. This happened under the eyes of one of the school boys who was alarmed to see me suddenly grow cold and lifeless and then cry out. I could not understand why this happened on the eve of my departure.

When night came, in the early a.m. hours of the 20th of August, Guruji again came to me, looking very young, with a great halo radiating from the right side of his face. As I was falling into *samadhi,* seeing him, he spoke: "Oh, don't go into the invisible when I am yet so visible." Then I asked, "Why do you look so young?" He replied, "This is how I used to look when I first started on this path. Now I can wear any garment of flesh I like. I thought you would like me in this new robe." When I praised his body, he said, "You are flattering me." There were a few saints with him, but I had no time to look at them, so deeply was I engrossed in Guru. Then I asked, "What brings you here, lord?" He replied, "Satan on this last day wanted to destroy your body that you might not be able to go to America and redeem other souls. I protected you and warned you. I came to explain what you did not understand." I had a grave suspicion as to the impending dangers before my departure hence; so I always wrote I shall leave here, God willing; and even now I say so as I sit preparing my departure on the *Naldera* August 22.

Oh, how I look forward to see you and the divine group at Mt. Washington. I am happiest you found my home at Mt. Washington your home. That makes it really our home. I always wished this, to make you happy somewhere in the divine company of guileless souls that has been my fortune to bring together and train with utmost carefulness. It takes a long time to iron out moods and discrepancies and bad karma from souls, wherein they become divinely natural and magnetic to all. It took lots of time, patience and labors, and soul-aches to make the children at Mt. Washington what they are. They are so different from the millions you meet, isn't it so? I knew some day you would know them and appreciate them....In heaven you shall be at my right and they on the left. This is the truth. I have seen that many times. A few others will be there too, but their names I shall withhold now....

I received your most joyous letter from Kansas City about your intending to visit Mt. Washington. I am happy beyond dreams that Mt. Washington has made you happy and drawn you there. My labors at Mt. Washington are worthwhile if it has given you even a moment's happiness.

God sometimes gives us more work than we can do; but if we believe, we are blessed with all the powers necessary to accomplish those tasks. There is no time element in God; whenever we believe in His power to work through us, it will work. First, we behold God as the doer and we His instruments. Later, we see He is the doer and He is the instrument.

The other day as I was coming in the train, I saw my body, the train, the sound, the tracks, the vast scenic tracts, melting into the Infinite. I asked, "What happened to me?" A voice said, "You were dreaming My dream of earth and of an earthly train travelling over it. Now your dream is over; you are awake in Me." I asked, "Naught exists but You—not the earth with all its complexities?" "No, they exist in a different way, much different from what people think about them. They exist in My dream only." Then the voice said, "Behold, I throw you into My dream, and you will behold your vast soul in the little body carried by a little bigger train over My little bigger earth, My tiny earth dream." Then all the noises and the quivering of the body from the movement of the train returned.

This wakeful state is a dream. Every night when we are awake in the invisibility of the peace of sleep and semi-soul contact, we realize this earth as a dream. Meditation is the conscious way of remaining in the empire of Omnipresence and Invisible Reality, so that we may falsify the audacious dream reality, or unreality, of this earth. Meditation is the way to stay in our real nature and forget our dream delusive nature of wakefulness. When we dream ourselves as limited human beings, the bones, flesh, good and bad sensations, pleasure, pain with death, riches, power, sickness, reincarnation, can all be seen in a dream. So stay in the Infinite constantly and forget this dream while doing everything for God and not for self.

Last of all, I cannot help telling you how considerate and how dear you are to me to satisfy me by stabilizing Ranchi headquarters just before my God-willing departure to see you all. May God give you untold power to do all the things you are doing. Many wish to do what you can do and are doing. How fortunate you are, and how happy I am that you are supremely happy in doing so, and in harmonizing with the Lord's will through me.

Hurrah! coming home. Reaching London September 11, 1936. Starting from London, October 3. Reaching New York October 8. Thence two days in Boston. Thence to Kansas City. Thence to Mt. Washington. A million blessings of my heart and soul for what you have done to please God, Gurus, and me; and thanks from all of India, Ranchi, and all India Yogodans. They all hail you as our Saint Lynn; and you shall be called in Heaven Saint Lynn throughout earth and eternity.

Eternal love and blessings to you and Mt. Washington blessed ones. Ever yours.

* * * * *

Sea Letter (Radiogram)
Aboard the *Naldera*
August 24, 1936

J. J. Lynn, Mount Washington Estates, Los Angeles, Calif.

Endless India's Yogodans' blessings for funds stabilizing Ranchi. Finally sailing towards dearest you, Mt. Washington, and all. Deepest joy, love.

* * * * *

Naldera
Port Said
August 30, 1936

Now you can't but believe that I am heading towards our America. Seems so many miles of water the poor ship has to swim over. But anyway we are nearing towards you, when I shall see your dearest face with childlike smile beaming with the halo of God. The starting was monotonous. I indulged in lapses of inner flights for hours. And now I have waked after a week of this continuous divine contact, waked in the sameness of ship life. So many superficial people around. Strange things happen to me. The Lord is showing me wherever I am that's my home. Somebody asked me on my way to Bombay, "Aren't you sad leaving India?" I replied, "My home is in the train now; then it shall be in the hotel; then in the ship. How can I leave my home? It is everywhere. I love India, I love America, yet the attachment for both has been taken away."

The best time of life is short, and there is much the Lord has given to you and me to accomplish. Isn't it wonderful that the Lord is commanding through me and making things possible through you. So many wish to do with me what you are doing, but you are the one chosen to do such wondrous things here. Yes, I know that gladness in doing God's work from the soul has visited your heart. Your second great battle is conquered. The third one you will be tested, and you will know when tested. I won't have to tell you. You have almost conquered; and when you will pass that test you will reach finality in this life. Seen or unseen I shall ever hover around you, guarding you with all my life in God unto the end. Keep thy faith ever and ever and ever increasing, for God through me is guiding you.

We are just reaching Port Said. It is getting late and I must dispatch this letter. We reach London Sept. 11, start for dear old America October 3, reaching about October 8. Please write me to London.

I am writing many things in Bengali and English, for now we must have books about our work and the Great Gurus. I must do a great deal of work as fast as I can; and we must do work together as fast as we can. It looks like India would need me again to complete the work we started. I am not showing impatience to return; but I met death twice in India (once in Bombay, as I wrote to you), and yet I love to work there in spite of threatening from Satan. As you go on, you consciously have to fight with the forces of evil by consciously using the power of God and the Gurus....

My earthly father who has been almost like my guru, almost expired. His life was trembling in the balance when I left. How can I thank you, O God's most beloved instrument, for being so indescribably good to me and the work. Remember, all my spiritual riches, everything I have, I have invisibly dedicated to you. Someday you will need them and know of my unending, unconditional, measureless love for you.

God catches my breast, and I feel the bounding of His boundless love, and I am bounding everywhere: that's why I must stop—

Ever taking you There where you and I are one. Deepest love to you and group. All Bengal and India loves you for Ranchi. Ever yours.

P.S. Again thank you for the immortal satisfaction of your listening to me and the Divine of your own accord. Our work together has filled my life. Such love as you have drawn from me none could; none have yet. This is from my heart, so please receive it as thus. I wrote a poem yesterday for us.

Two Names

We work for God now,
And shall work for Him anon through two names.
Though the body shall sleep one day,
And we no more incarnate shall be,
Yet will we leave our convincing fame
To work through our names.
Our unseen souls shall wear the frames
Of two glorious names
And work in the world
Without the body gross.
Our voices shall be silent,
But we shall ever be speaking, eloquent

Paramahansa Yogananda with Rajarsi Janakananda, Sri Daya Mata, Dr. M. W. Lewis and some of the other disciples and friends who had gathered at the SRF International Headquarters to welcome him home after his eighteen-month trip to Europe and India.

Through our works, books, and writings.
Though our minds shall leave the bondage of the brain,
Still we shall have made records of our minds
In the pages of our work and lived lives;
Those records will sing our songs of truth
To whomsoever will play them
With the needles of their minds.
We shall no more sing His name through our mortal voices,
But sing His name we shall
Through our bodiless names.
We care not who praises us
Or casts o'er us the gloom of blame:
Praise won't make us better, nor blame make us a whit less;
We are what we are.
We work for God now, and we will work for Him anon
Through two names.
We know He loves us, and we love Him.
That's all we want to sing anyway
Through eternity, silently, day by day—
And loudly, if we happen in people's minds to frame
And there hold the pictures of our good names.

When our body ceases
The good we do oft closes.
But we can live in names
In peoples' memory's frames
And continue to do useful good
To those lost on their way.

If names can thus work after us, why not have a name.
Let us be up and doing
Not just for the joy of having a name
But that our names we leave behind us

Can continue helping those who need us.
Oh, let us now acquire through mighty deeds a name
That will live in public fancy's frame
That long behind us our good names
Can work without the fleshly frames.

Paramahansa Yogananda and Mr. Lynn, on grounds of SRF Hermitage, Encinitas, California, 1940. Paramahansaji said: "Mr. Lynn and I live in the greatest joy and friendship. What I expected of him in spiritual development, he has more than fulfilled. He represents the best in American business principles as well as in universal spiritual principles."

Mr. Lynn's Words About Paramahansa Yogananda and the Self-Realization Path

In 1937 Mr. Lynn attended an SRF banquet given in Los Angeles, California, to celebrate the return of Paramahansaji from his eighteen-month trip to India and Europe. The following speech by Mr. Lynn was given on January 3, 1937.

Just five years ago I had the great privilege of meeting Paramahansa Yogananda for the first time. I had always been interested in truth and religion, although I had never accepted any church. My life was business; but my soul was sick and my body was decaying and my mind was disturbed. I was so nervous I couldn't sit still.

An Experience of the Healing Light

After I had met Paramahansaji and had been with him a little while, I became aware that I was sitting very still; I was motionless; I didn't seem to be breathing. I wondered about it and looked up at Paramahansaji. A deep white light appeared, seeming to fill the entire room. I became a part of that wondrous light. Since that time I have been free from nervousness.

I found that I had discovered something real, something immensely valuable to me. I had had to be sure. Not until my experience of the healing light did I realize that I had found entrance into a spiritual realm previously unknown to me.

The beautiful thing in these teachings is that one doesn't have to depend on blind beliefs. He experiences. He *knows* he knows, because he experiences. Ordinarily man is conscious only of his thoughts and of the material world that he can smell, taste, touch, see, and hear. But he is not conscious of the soul deep within him that makes it possible for him to think and to cognize the outer world through his senses. He doesn't know anything about That which is behind the scenes, just behind the thoughts and senses. One should learn to realize the presence of this Life, the real Life; and attain the union of his own consciousness with that Life.

Wealth Without Wisdom Cannot Give Joy

Before I met Paramahansaji the thought had not occurred to me that man could be conscious to a fuller extent than I was at that time. Yet, having enjoyed the things of the world, I had come to a point of distress; because, as I said a moment ago, my soul was sick and my body was not well. Nothing seemed to satisfy me. If you have had an opportunity to observe the rich, those with vast possessions, you have found that most of them are discontented and unhappy. Wealth without wisdom cannot give joy. All of us are seeking joy in life; in everything we do we are seeking happiness.

Self-Realization Path—A Blend of Yoga and Devotion

On the path of Self-Realization one becomes alive again. He actually lives. He feels the divine Life within him. He experiences the union of his individual soul with the universal Spirit. The Self-Realization path as taught by Paramahansaji is scientific. It is a combination of yoga—a science that is practiced within one's own being—and devotion to God. Together, yoga and devotion will bring man to a realization of his own divinity.

Religion can have but one purpose: knowledge of one's own life as the omnipresent Life. That attainment is Heaven. From my own experience I am firmly of this opinion: without making a successful effort to achieve soul-realization, man cannot win salvation or final freedom in Spirit.

A Combination Needed of Western and Eastern Treasures

America is rich in material accomplishments. And India is rich in the wisdom of Spirit. A combination of the two will lead to an ideal world-civilization.

One who lives in the material world alone, in the consciousness of materiality, is attached to possessions. Attachment develops slavery. We become slaves to habits and possessions. It is not possessions that make us slaves, but ignorance and attachment.

One with material attachments is never free. He has placed his faith in things that he is bound to lose. Only one possession is lasting: Spirit. Take the Spirit out of anything and it has no attraction at all. Life is truly Spirit.

Two things stay with us when the body goes: life and consciousness. We can get rid of everything except life and consciousness. Those are eternally with us. Self-Realization Fellowship teachings show one how to develop a proper consciousness—an awareness and inner experience of Spirit.

Paramahansaji doesn't ask his students to accept anything as a matter of belief only. "Practice *Kriya Yoga*," he says, "and discover for yourself the glories of the soul within."

Paramahansaji, Embodiment of Love

A master is like an angel of God. In our beloved Paramahansaji we have one who is the very embodiment of love and unselfishness. He is the possessor of divine joy. His contact goes back to a chain of illumined Masters.* To the Western mind this statement may sound a little strange, but it is true. The Masters are linked, one with another. They have contact with the Spirit, and through their powers that Spirit is transmitted to other men. What a blessing it has been for us that India (a country that many people think of as a land of snake charmers) sent to our shores a master who can help us to achieve God-consciousness.

Those who commune with Spirit know a beauty, a sweetness, that is not experienced in any other way.

How heavenly it is to enjoy the company of a saint! Of all the things that have come to me in life, I treasure more than all else the blessings Paramahansaji has bestowed on me.

The Ancient Hindus Developed a Soul Science

I must admit I was prejudiced at first. Once I was one of those who thought of Hindus as snake charmers. Now I revere India as the land whose saints develop the highest of all sciences—yoga, the techniques for soul-exploration.

* * * * *

Extracts from a speech delivered by Mr. Lynn, January 8, 1938, Encinitas, California, at the first anniversary celebration of the founding of Self-Realization Fellowship Ashram Center in Encinitas.

I would rather keep silent than say very much. I would rather feel and realize than talk. But today I would like to tell you a little bit about the blessings that come to one from Self-Realization Fellowship teachings. The first blessing is calmness. We cannot have peace with-

* See page 184.

out poise. In 1932, when I first met Paramahansa Yogananda, I was afflicted with extreme nervousness. Since that time one of the greatest joys that has come into my life is serenity. Everyone, I now know, can be calm and peaceful.

As a boy I lived in the country. I had some hound dogs whose sense of smell was very keen. Every time they smelled the game they were tracking they would give a yelp. That is how people of the world act—those who live in the senses: they give a yelp whenever they have sensations of pain or pleasure. They have not learned that true life and joy do not depend on sensory experiences. We must find the source of happiness and joy. And that source is God.

The Blessings of Self-Realization Fellowship Teachings

Another great blessing that comes to the SRF devotee is physical and mental health. If our minds are unsettled and uncontrolled, eventually our bodies will be disturbed. We will burn up energy faster than we can receive it. Our minds will be like the inconstant flicker of a candle. In that state we cannot be peaceful or happy or calm. Until we release our minds from a sense of constant strain, we are unable to enjoy true health.

We think our life depends on breath. We believe we have got to be breathing all the time. In a room where the air is not fresh we get sleepy and lose our energy. But an SRF yogi learns how to calm and control the breath. How wonderful it is to be able to sit perfectly still without breath and to live directly on the cosmic energy that is all about us and within us! If that is not a blessing which a man should give his life to find and enjoy, I don't know what anyone could rightly call a blessing!

Consciousness is the one thing that we can never get away from. It is the one thing that is ours and that nobody can deprive us of. It is the gift of our Creator. It is God Himself residing within us.

India has concentrated on understanding the consciousness of man. The right state of consciousness, devotion to God, and following *Kriya Yoga* technique as brought to us from India are a sure way to happiness. In a very short time the teachings of Paramahansa Yogananda can make a greater contribution to our lives—health, happiness, peace of mind, and realization of the fullness of our being—than can all the comforts offered by the developments of material science.

The baby is the son of Yoshio Hamada, Japanese gardener at the SRF Hermitage in Encinitas. The child's name is James Lynn Hamada.

The superintendent at Lynn Farms, Borrego Springs, was a Japanese, George Shintaku. Imbued with great reverence for his employer, George would present himself, freshly bathed, every evening at Mr. Lynn's door for a *darshan* (the blessing that one receives in gazing on a saint).

Man is not God, but God is in man. The sooner we realize that He dwells in us the sooner we come to the realization of what our real life is. We have an urge for something higher; we don't know what it is. But it is an urge for happiness and joy—happiness that lies within us. We cannot find it until we discover it within the soul.

Honor Due India for Her Spiritual Investigations

India, in the person of one of her great masters, Paramahansa Yogananda, has brought to us this priceless knowledge of soul-realization. How grateful we should be to a people whose greatest men, down through the centuries, have given their lives, have renounced everything else, in order to explore the divine potentialities in man! What India has given us today in Paramahansaji's teachings is worth more to us than anything we could give India in exchange. Today the Western man is in dire need of a spiritual technique for developing his soul resources. That technique is *Kriya Yoga,* an ancient science brought to us for the first time by a Master from India.

If everything man can possess is outside of him, and if everything that creates impressions on him comes from outside, could he be said to have a true "life" of his own? He must go within to find true life.

"I Have Learned to Live by Inward Joy"

Those of us who are open-minded enough and sincere enough to investigate the truths that Paramahansaji exemplifies are certainly the most blessed people of America. I see that—from my own experience. From following the SRF teachings I have received calmness, peace, joy, wisdom, and all the other blessings of life. No longer does it make much difference whether or not I have anything from the external world; I have learned to live by inward joy. It is the most beautiful thing that life can offer.

After you have reached that state of soul happiness, you can melt yourself into Spirit—a blissful state beyond the finite comprehension. And that joy is the one thing that we are all in search of; it is the one possession that man pursues from life to life. Wherever he goes he will search for that divine happiness. That ever new Joy is God. It comes by one's own Self-realization. And when a man attains Self-realization he naturally has fellowship with his brothers, because he knows he is one with all.

Mr. Lynn on beach at Encinitas, 1937. He said: "In the knowledge and wisdom that Paramahansa Yogananda brings to us we are able to realize, consciously feel, and know unshakably that our soul is one with Spirit. What greater blessing, what greater assurance could one have?"

May I ask that all of you stand as a tribute to our Paramahansa Yogananda? We are paying homage to the great soul that resides in the body sitting here. But he is not confined to a fleshly frame. That is just the state in which we see him with our physical eyes. If our hearts are receptive we glimpse much more in him than we can see and touch with the senses. If our consciousness is attuned to spiritual truths we perceive in him something that is beyond the power of the senses to detect: the Divine Life.

I appreciate your getting up to pay tribute to this great man, this spiritual teacher who has the wisdom that "surpasseth understanding."

* * * * *

The following are extracts from a talk given by Mr. Lynn at an SRF gathering in Los Angeles, California, on January 18, 1940.

The perfect fulfillment we are all seeking will come to us through Self-realization. And what is Self-realization? Consciousness of God— inner perception that your very life is God. That awakening or awareness will come to you when you are able to contact God through the teachings of a true guru. Jesus said, "I do nothing of myself."* He gave the credit to God. The man of wisdom claims nothing for himself; he is without ego. He realizes that God is the only One that does anything. His alone is the Power.

In the SRF path we don't give up anything worthwhile. We actually find that for which we have been constantly searching. We will never be content until our deepest search is rewarded. It is through the teachings and blessings of a master, our Master, that we may receive that which we seek.

Our Business Duties May Be Carried on Harmoniously

If we are at peace within our beings, we can harmoniously carry on our duties even in the business sphere. We can accomplish admirable things in the world without necessarily clashing with others. After our day's work is over we can retire within to be with God again. Eventually, even in the business world, we can perform all our duties with the full consciousness of God's presence. If we are calm and peaceful,

* John 8:28.

Rajarsi Janakananda at Borrego Springs, 1954. Of him, Paramahansa Yogananda said: "I am proud that in Mr. Lynn a Westerner stepped forth to show the world the worth in daily life of yoga training. Through him the lives of many, many men will be profoundly changed and turned toward God."

come what may—success or seeming failure—we remain even-minded, feeling the certainty that His will is being done.

If we could gain the whole world, and have nothing else but the world, we would not find happiness. Earthly possessions cannot bestow peace and joy. *God can.*

Divine consciousness is That which is the essential part of our being. It is possible to realize That. It is possible to experience It. We don't have to take anyone else's word for it. We may realize ourselves as partaking in the life of God Himself. We need not separate ourselves from Him.

After one has experienced the divine consciousness, he enjoys it immeasurably more than he enjoys anything else. *I have found that nothing the world can give me is comparable to the joy in meditation and the consciousness of God's presence.*

We have to make the effort ourselves. But if we allow our will to be led by the wisdom of a master whose will is in tune with God's, the master then seeks to guide our will in such a way that we travel swiftly on the road back to divinity. The chief difference between a worldly man and a saint is that the wise man has attuned his will to the Divine Will.

We say that God is omnipresent. The word omnipresent has only a vague meaning for most people. Could it be otherwise when they must imagine it only? Imagination cannot convey the sense of omnipresence; only experience can do that. True spiritual experience is realization of the very presence within us of the Infinite God.

We don't have to feel that the consciousness of Jesus was different from that of any God-illumined master of India. The real master, whether in India or in this country or anywhere else, is he who is one with God. He has united his soul with Him. The power he manifests is simply the divine current flowing through him.

All Illumined Men Live in the Same Divine Consciousness

After soul-realization we may read all scriptures understandingly. Otherwise we don't get the true significance of words of the prophets. You will find that all scriptures confirm the teachings of every great master. The Bibles of the world confirm everything that Self-Realization Fellowship undertakes to teach us. There is no essential difference.

Paramahansaji and Mr. Lynn playing with a toy airplane, a Christmas gift from Guru to disciple, on a porch at the Hermitage, Encinitas, 1947.

Mr. Lynn, 1947. He was close to Nature; healthful sunbaths in the privacy of the Hermitage grounds were a daily feature of his visits to Encinitas. His was truly a balanced life—the ideal of the sages. He was successful in the business world and on the spiritual path. He never neglected his body; for its sake he formed every good habit of diet, outdoor living, and physical exercise as taught by Paramahansaji.

It is within the power of every one of us to attain true wisdom. We have to make the effort. It is up to us. We must meditate to attain deep faith. After we have received the first contact of God, we should then seek to develop the contact into a greater and greater consciousness. That is what Jesus asked everyone to do. He wanted them to receive his omnipresent consciousness. And that is what Paramahansaji teaches. He brings us God and all he asks is that we receive.

May you tune your will to God's will and make the effort to attain Self-realization! When you have found the teachings that can bring you to God, accept them. Know your Heavenly Father and enjoy His glory.

*   *   *   *   *

Mr. Lynn made the following speech on February 20, 1948. The occasion was the annual Flower Show in Encinitas, California, where some of the finest perfume-essence flowers in America are grown. The SRF gardens in Encinitas were represented at the Show with a display of cyclamens, caladiums, hydrangeas, and cinerarias. Later in the day Mr. Lynn spoke again at the unveiling of three towers, erected along the main thoroughfare to mark the grounds of the Encinitas Ashram Center.

Most people go through life wondering what it is all about. They know many things, but little about themselves. All human beings are created under divine law; but if they are ignorant of the divine laws, they know little if anything about how life should be lived. We assume at times to understand a great deal. When we think we know a lot, that is the time that each of us had better ask himself: "Do I know anything about my real Self?"

Man in His Human Aspect Cannot Find Happiness

We go through life expecting to get our pleasures from the outward world, from the money we make, from the things we build up—but all of these perish. Therefore, in the innermost depths of our hearts, we are dissatisfied. We find at times that, after all, we are not so big. We don't amount to so much. When we take a true inventory of ourselves, free from vanity, we find that we are a very insignificant particle of life.

And so I am grateful that in my progress through life I found Paramahansa Yogananda. When I met him I was a man very busy with many affairs. I thought I had accumulated some of the worthwhile things of life; yet I was not happy. I had found that everything I obtained lost its value. When I had obtained it, its attraction disappeared. I could not be happy, and yet I went along as best I could. I never thought that someday I would find a great teacher who would give me an understanding of my Self.

The Blessings I Have Found Through Paramahansaji

One of the blessings I have received in my friendship with Paramahansa Yogananda has been permanent relief from a state of nervousness, a state of strain, an inward state of uncertainty. I have gained calmness, peace, joy, and a sense of security that cannot come to anyone until he has found the true security of the soul. Paramahansaji has brought me this understanding, this blessing of knowledge of the law of man's real being.

As I walked through the flower show today I thought of the flowers as one of the greatest creations of God. In them we find beauty, color, and perfume. But the loveliness of the soul is greater than the beauty of the flower. Yet the soul cannot be known in its vast and glorious na-

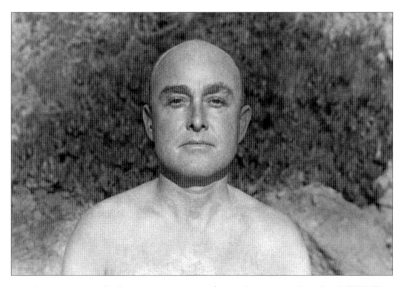

Mr. Lynn in *samadhi* (superconsciousness), on the private beach of SRF Hermitage, Encinitas, California, January 1937. "I have found," he said, "that nothing the world can give me is comparable to the joy of meditation and the consciousness of God's presence."

ture, cannot express itself in a man's daily life, so long as he remains in ignorance of himself.

Man is an intelligent being, a wonderful being; but he must be conscious of himself, of his true nature. When our consciousness is limited to the senses we are not aware of our real being.

Yoga Is the Science of the Soul

Yoga is the science by which one unites his soul with Spirit. A yogi is one who employs definite meditation techniques in order to realize his true nature of soul, united forever with the Absolute Spirit, or God. Without such knowledge of the soul, we are not capable of understanding the laws under which God has created us.

In the knowledge and wisdom that Paramahansa Yogananda brings to us we are able to attain a true consciousness of the meaning of our own life. We are able to realize, consciously feel, and know unshakably that our soul is one with Spirit. What greater blessing, what greater assurance could one have?

*   *   *   *   *

After the passing of Paramahansa Yogananda on March 7, 1952, Mr. Lynn assumed the presidency of SRF/YSS and was thereafter called "Rajarsi Janakananda," the name Guruji had chosen for him. Rajarsi gave the following talk at India Hall, Hollywood, California, on April 7, 1952. The occasion was a banquet, attended by 250 Self-Realization students, celebrating the first anniversary of India Hall. The structure was designed by the Guru and built in 1951 by SRF members.

I am going to address you as the children of God, the children of Master, of the God that is in Master. Our Guru came out of the East to the West to bring us, by the example of his life and by his spoken and written words, a divine message of conscious union with God. It was the Heavenly Father who chose Master, incarnated him, and sent him to America, that he might bring us all closer to Him.

Who Is a Master?

A master is not a master of somebody else; he is the master of himself. That is the truth we should recognize. We should be masters of ourselves. Even God does not try to master others. He has given us life, consciousness, and free will to live the divine life if we choose. We cannot live in peace or perfection without a sense of our oneness with God.

All Masters Speak the Same Truth

The Christian scriptures give us the same teachings that Master brought to us. The words of all true Sons reveal the One Father.

For those of us who will make the effort, there is still the same opportunity to receive from Master the same consciousness, the same love that was here when he was present with us in the body. Since his passing our awareness of him has increased many times. We should not feel that there has been any loss. I have found the feeling, the realization, the power of his cosmic consciousness to be so great as to be overwhelming.

We are still able to be in communion with Master in spirit; he is with us and is manifesting Life. Do you think that God would send him and then completely withdraw him from us? Surely the Lord does not work that way.* Master's coming here was the work of God, for he was chosen by Him to spread the yoga message in the West.

Paramahansaji the Guru of This Path

Master is our guru. There will be no other guru. Is there another preceptor? He will continue as always to be our preceptor.

* * * * *

Rajarsi presided at the 1952 Convocation, which marked the 32nd anniversary of Self-Realization Fellowship in America. On July 26th, at the Mt. Washington headquarters in Los Angeles, California, Rajarsi gave Kriya Yoga initiation to 400 members. Extracts from his speech at the Convocation on July 27, 1952, are given below.

My subject is the soul. You may think of the soul as a vague "something." But do you feel it? Do you realize it? Can you be That and not an ego? Can you be That and not a mind? Can you be beyond mind? These questions cannot be answered truly except by those who have discovered by meditation the existence of the soul within.

The soul is a reflection of Spirit. The Absolute God the Father is beyond all creation; we are His myriad reflections in creation. Because God

---

* "And I will pray the Father, and He shall give you another Comforter [*Aum*], that He may abide with you forever, even the Spirit of truth....I will not leave you comfortless: I will come to you. Yet a little while, and the world seeth me no more; but ye see me; because I live, ye shall live also. At that day ye shall know that I am in my Father, and ye in me, and I in you."—John 14:16–20.

is a reflection of Himself in each one of us, we can be many, yet all one Father, one Life. And if indeed we are reflections of God, we cannot be only mortal beings. We must be immortal.

But each of us has the power to act as a mortal being or as a god, because God gave us the free choice. When we do our will and not His will, when we act as mortals rather than as His divine children, we violate our own being. And then we must naturally suffer the sad consequences.

What every soul really wants is simply to become one with Spirit. We yearn to be that Life, that Joy, that Love which Master brings to us. Even when I say anything about that Life I feel the presence of Master. He is here! It is impossible for me to speak without feeling this joy of Master's presence. He is not a body; he is not a mind. He is Spirit. He is Life.

I don't care to talk much. I enjoy being this Life, this Spirit, this reflection of God that Master brings to us. He is right here. Master is this joy that I feel. Master brings us this joy, this great power of Spirit. That love of Master's—that love surpassing human understanding—is the love of God. That love is ours. That love is Spirit.

Follow the Plan That Master Taught

You should follow the techniques, the suggestions, the plan, the way that Master brought and gave to you to take you away from the ego, to relieve you from the consciousness of the burdensome body and from the restless mind; to take you into Spirit, into God. Be one with That.

The greatest sin is ignorance—ignorance of the Divine. But you may discover for yourself this joy, this love of Master's, of Spirit. No love was ever so great, so joyful; and he is pouring this love into you. Receive it! You must learn his way, and develop your insight. Know the Power that Master is manifesting. It is real. It is not a matter of imagination or of mere intellectual speculation. It is the eternal foundation of your true being. You must know it. Master brings you the way. When you receive him you will lift yourself into the light, the grace, the wisdom of God.

* * * * *

Rajarsi and Paramahansa Yogananda in pulpit of Self-Realization Fellowship Church of All Religions, Hollywood, California, 1942. Whenever Mr. Lynn would arrive in Los Angeles from Kansas City, Paramahansaji would garland the disciple in the Indian fashion.

In a talk at the SRF Church in Hollywood on April 7, 1952, Rajarsi said: "I am going to address you as the children of God, the children of Master, of the God that is in Master. Our Guru came out of the East to the West to bring us, by the example of his life and by his spoken and written words, a divine message of conscious union with God. It was the Heavenly Father that chose Paramahansaji, incarnated him, and sent him to America, that he might bring us all closer to Him."

The following was Rajarsi's Christmas message in 1952 to all members of Self-Realization Fellowship/Yogoda Satsanga Society of India.

With deep joy in my heart I extend greetings to you at this blessed Christmas season. Seldom before have men so needed to experience the true meaning of Christmas—consciously to receive in their hearts the omnipresent love, the joy, the peace of the Christ Consciousness that we celebrate in the coming of Jesus.

Through the blessings of the Masters and our guru Paramahansa Yogananda, and through their Self-Realization Fellowship teachings, my eyes have been opened to the inner spiritual beauty of this season; my heart has been filled with the great love of the omnipresent Christ.

It is my humble wish to share with you this divine love and joy. In our hearts and minds let us gather around the Christmas tree of the world and pray with Jesus Christ and our Gurus that their message of peace, forgiveness, and love to all mankind fall on receptive ears. May all peoples awaken to the light of truth and understanding! Let every heart sing with the angelic chorus, "Glory to God in the highest, and on earth peace, good will toward men."

* * * * *

The following message from Rajarsi was read to Self-Realization Fellowship center leaders at the Convocation in Los Angeles, August 1953.

To you, the center leaders, I am deeply grateful for the wonderful way in which you are holding aloft the torch of Self-Realization that was first set alight in this land by our incomparable guru Paramahansa Yogananda.

High Responsibility of Center Leaders

Our center leaders are entrusted with a very special privilege and divine responsibility. All of you, I know, are striving to express in your daily lives the perfect conduct and high ideals that our beloved Master taught by precept and by lifelong example. Let your light so shine before worldly men that they will be inspired to emulate you and thus to regenerate their own lives through *Kriya Yoga.*

To serve as center leaders for the pioneering spiritual movement of Self-Realization Fellowship is not always easy, but the reward is great. God bless you all! I will close with a quotation from our ever-living guru Paramahansaji. On March 6, 1952—one day before that of his fi-

Mr. Lynn in *samadhi* (superconsciousness), summer of 1936. The site of two meditation caves facing the Pacific Ocean was being dug on the grounds of the newly built SRF Hermitage, Encinitas, California.

"No longer does it make much difference whether or not I have anything from the external world," Mr. Lynn said. "I have learned to live by inward joy. It is the most beautiful thing that life can offer."

nal *samadhi*—he addressed a group of Self-Realization residents and teachers at Mt. Washington. He told them:

"If other men and women fool away their time, *you* be lost in God. You will go ahead. *Prepare yourself. This work will spread all over the world.* Love people with divine love, and be only with those that love the Lord. Let your example be the way to change others' lives. Reform yourself and you will reform thousands. Egotism is the hardest thing to overcome. Don't think of yourself. When people say good things about you, give the credit to God. Love Him; cry for Him. What does anything else matter? Throw yourself into God, be filled with His love and joy."

*   *   *   *   *

At the garden party on Mt. Washington Estates, Self-Realization head-quarters, that concluded the 1953 Convocation, Rajarsi addressed the students. The following is an excerpt from his speech.

Rajarsi *(in front of tree)* presiding over the Christmas Day banquet for monks and nuns of the Self-Realization Order, 1953, Mt. Washington international headquarters, Los Angeles

All that I have to give you is the spirit of Master and of God. I have nothing more to say, nothing more to do except to carry out the wishes that Master had for this great movement. And what he is doing for you these days is not of me. I myself am only his "little one" that he spoke of; and I shall never be more than a little one because it will always be Master, Paramahansaji, who is my life and my blessing to you all.

* * * * *

Rajarsi was the host at a dinner on Thanksgiving Day, 1953, at the Hermitage in Encinitas, California. About fifty SRF devotees attended. The following are excerpts from his speech on that occasion.

Understand That God Is the Only Reality

It is a great blessing, through Master's grace, to have realized myself to be not merely a body but an immortal soul. And someday that will be your own blessing: when you do not identify your Self with the body but know your true nature of Spirit. When you melt into God you will understand that He is the only Reality.

Master is here, just behind the darkness of our closed eyes. Receive the blessing that he gives you even now, and melt with him into the ocean of God's joy. Master wants us to be happy, and he is always with us. Tune in with him and you will never be without the bliss, the love, the peace of God.

* * * * *

Meditation services are held annually in all Self-Realization Fellowship temples, ashrams, and centers on January 5th to commemorate Paramahansaji's birthday. Rajarsi spent January 5, 1954, in seclusion at his retreat in Borrego Springs, California. Later he recounted to other disciples of Gurudeva the following sublime experience.

A Sacred Experience With Master in the Other World

I awoke around two or three o'clock in the morning on January 5th, and saw Lahiri Mahasaya in the greatest blaze of light in which he has ever manifested to me. Then, one by one, Sri Yukteswar, Babaji, and Master appeared. Master lifted me out of the body and we floated together over many gatherings of people. Master blessed each group as we floated over it. We were not walking, but floating overhead. It seemed as though Master wanted all the people to know that I was with him.

I was with Master a long time, from two or three o'clock until nine o'clock—the longest I have ever been with him in this way.

Master is very busy there, just as busy as he was when he lived here—helping the people in those other spheres, teaching them the way of salvation and how to achieve their own Self-realization.

* * * * *

The 1954 Convocation, held in August in Los Angeles, marked the 34th anniversary of Self-Realization Fellowship in America. The 400 students who attended the Convocation came from twenty-two states of America and from nine foreign countries. On this occasion the following message from Rajarsi was read.

The purpose of these Convocations is to bring sincere seekers of truth together for what our guru, Paramahansa Yogananda, called "fellowship with God through Self-realization." This, Master said, is the true significance of the name Self-Realization Fellowship. To followers of this path, therefore, "fellowship" means more than the harmonious feeling engendered when men of like mind gather together to discuss ideas and ideals. To Self-Realization members "fellowship" signifies the blissful sense of universal oneness that comes with the recognition, through meditation, of the individual soul's kinship with the Father and Friend of all.

How True Brotherhood May Be Attained

Divine fellowship is necessary before men can know true brotherhood and its natural sequel—peace on earth. The blessed Master was sent to this world to help mankind to understand how to live in fellowship with God and thereby in human brotherhood and true happiness.

You have only to follow the way that Master has shown, with steadfast zeal and devotion, and you will find God. You will realize then, as I do now, that Master is here at this very moment, with you, and with me. Attune yourself that you may know in your soul that Master is here. When Master comes to you, you will realize that nothing exists for you except the love of God; that nothing else is so important to you as His love. Master has melted my soul with his into God. Receive his blessing! Perceive the light of God, and, in it, Master's greatness.

RAJARSI OFFICIATED AT PARAMAHANSAJI'S FUNERAL

Rajarsi conducted the last rites for Paramahansa Yogananda at the headquarters on March 11, 1952. At the start of the services a rainbow appeared in the skies. In a beautiful speech at the bier, Rajarsi said: "Master gave us his love as father, mother, and friend. His whole life, his whole expression, his whole satisfaction was in the giving of that great love. How outstandingly great, outstandingly gracious, outstandingly kind he was!"

The Ambassador of India, Dr. Binay Ranjan Sen *(center)*, spoke at the funeral. His eulogy of Yogananda ended with the words: "Death has no victory in him."

The Ambassador's closing words were singularly prophetic. For weeks after Yogananda's death his unchanged face shone with the divine luster of incorruptibility. Manifesting a phenomenal state of immutability, his body emanated no odor of decay. In death, as in life, the great yogi demonstrated the power of Spirit over matter. (The full testimony by Mr. Harry T. Rowe, mortuary director at Forest Lawn Memorial-Park, appears in the booklet, *Paramahansa Yogananda: In Memoriam.*)

The following are a few words of welcome from Rajarsi to Self-Realization students at a Convocation in August 1954, Los Angeles.

Master through me welcomes you to the 1954 SRF Convocation. This two-in-oneness is not just an idea or an expression of mine; through Master's grace my soul has melted into his, and we are one in God. Master expresses himself through the humble instrument of this body and mind. But Master would never say that any credit belonged to him—he acknowledged only God as the Doer. God is working through Master, through the Great Ones, that all of us may enjoy, by right action and right meditation, oneness with Him; that we may melt, even as the Masters have done, into the bliss of Spirit.

Remember, as you attend the Convocation classes and join in the other spiritual activities that have been planned for you, that Master is here. He is just behind the darkness of closed eyes when we sit to meditate. He is watching and waiting for us as we put forth that steadfast, daily, ever-deepening effort in meditation that makes it possible for him to lift us up to God. He wants us to be happy in the knowledge that he is always here with us. Discovering this, in deepest meditation, we will discover also the joy, the peace, the love of God.

A LITTLE BIRTHDAY GIFT

By Paramahansa Yogananda

(Written for Rajarsi in 1939 on his birthday, May 5th)

Into the cradle of my love
Came a little one from above:
An image of love divine,
Of humbleness, understanding, will adamantine.

That day the earth was blessed:
An ideal child adorned her breast,
To be an example after my dreams;
To know and show others: "Earth is not what it seems."

The saintly little one, sitting
On an altar of grass, meditating;
Enshrined by a temple of sky and sun,
Thinking of only one—the Only One.

Could more joy I feel
Than in beholding his soul with the seal
Of mine own and the Great Ones' complete content,
In this path of divine intent?

When such a one awoke in God's love
Flowers unseen rained from above
Not here only; but in the lightland
Of India, blessed by the Astral Dove.

Guruji (*right*) holds in his hand a gift-card, whose message he reads aloud to Mr. Lynn. The beloved disciple is opening a Christmas gift from Paramahansaji. Photo taken in Guruji's study in the Encinitas Hermitage, 1944.

Eulogies at Rajarsi's Funeral

On February 20, 1955, Rajarsi Janakananda entered mahasamadhi *at his retreat in Borrego Springs, California. The funeral service in Los Angeles, California, was held at Forest Lawn Memorial-Park in the hall called "Church of the Recessional" at 10 a.m., February 23, 1955.*

On this occasion Sri Daya Mata, president of SRF/YSS since March 7, 1955, gave the following moving talk.

Dear ones, please forgive me if my voice breaks with emotion this morning. This occasion, for us and for the world, is a solemn one. We of Self-Realization Fellowship have lost the physical presence of a beloved saint, our revered president; the world has lost one of its most eminent sons.

It was in 1932 that Master traveled to Kansas City to give a series of lectures and classes. There he met Mr. Lynn—the devotee who later became Rajarsi Janakananda. In 1933 Mr. Lynn visited the Los Angeles headquarters for the first time. An incident took place then that has remained in my memory all these years. One evening Master called me to his kitchen and asked me to bring him a needle and a spool of black thread. He was holding a pair of suspenders. When I had brought the requested articles he began to sew up a rent in the suspenders. I quickly offered to do the work, but he replied: "Oh, no, I will fix these myself. Can you imagine! Mr. Lynn has worn these same suspenders for ten years." Master was filled with delight and affection, realizing that although Mr. Lynn could have purchased almost anything, he had lived so simply that one pair of suspenders had been worn and mended over a period of ten years.

This incident left an indelible impression on my mind. Truly Rajarsi was one of those great devotees who had learned to live "in the world, but not of it." His simplicity was untouched by the material success he had achieved. He was the most humble of men, his mind ever remaining fixed on God.

My mind recalls another inspiring picture that I want to share with you: a picture of those two lovers of God, one the Master, one the disciple—him whom Paramahansaji called his "little one" and his "most blessed beloved little one."

A slight smile of ineffable peace was on Rajarsi's face as he lay in his casket at the funeral on February 23, 1955. The pile of rose leaves (*extreme right*) was a tribute from hundreds of Self-Realization members and friends in Los Angeles who filed past the casket, dropping rose petals.

Some of the floral tributes at Rajarsi's funeral, Forest Lawn Memorial-Park, Los Angeles, February 23, 1955. The beloved second president died of pneumonia on February 20th in Borrego Springs.

During those times when Master and Rajarsi were in Encinitas together, every evening they could be seen walking, hand in hand, up and down the flagstone path on the lawn in back of the Hermitage. Their eyes would be shining with the love and friendship they shared with God and with each other. We younger disciples would race to the windows at eventide to watch those two divine children as they strolled along. Sometimes Master would be speaking about some deep philosophical subject, and then his "little one" would remain quiet, listening intently. At other times both would be silent, absorbed in the inner bliss.

Seldom has the world seen such a perfect friendship. Observing them together, we were often reminded of the beautiful relationship of St. Francis and St. Dominic.

Few men have reached the heights of material success attained by Rajarsi; fewer still, particularly in the West, have reached the great spiritual heights scaled by him. It is remarkable indeed when one man is able to ascend to the top of both those peaks!

The world will soon forget the business accomplishments of Mr. Lynn, but the name of Rajarsi Janakananda will be immortalized for the great services he rendered to Self-Realization Fellowship; and, above all, for his spiritual splendor and sweetness that helped everyone around him to realize more fully the beauty of the Divine Beloved that absorbed his whole being.

The following eulogy was delivered at Rajarsi's funeral by Rev. M. W. Lewis, then vice president of Self-Realization Fellowship.

We are unable to pay adequate tribute with words to such a noble and exalted soul as James J. Lynn, known to most of us as Rajarsi Janakananda. He lived engrossed in the light and love of the Infinite Father, an illumination bestowed on him through the channel of our beloved Master Paramahansa Yogananda. Only with the language of our hearts may we pay fitting tribute to Rajarsi. And that language is the unconditional divine love we feel for him.

II Corinthians 4:18 reads: "We look not at the things which are seen, but at the things which are not seen: for the things which are seen are temporal; but the things which are not seen are eternal."

No one understood this wisdom better than our beloved Rajarsi. As proof we have his exemplary life. He was a great organizer, a keen

SRI DAYA MATA

The Reverend Mother Daya Mata has been president and spiritual head of
Self-Realization Fellowship/Yogoda Satsanga Society of India since 1955
(succeeding Rajarsi Janakananda, the second president).

businessman; yet in the face of present-day tensions he somehow found the time daily to merge himself in the light and love of God and his Guru. Rajarsi often said: "Since meeting Master I have found the peace and bliss that supersedes all else."

In II Corinthians 5:1 we find the words: "For we know that if our earthly house of this tabernacle were dissolved, we have a building of God, an house not made with hands, eternal in the heavens." Rajarsi knew that "building of God," that "house eternal in the heavens." He once said: "I am a free soul, unlimited by the body-consciousness; I am free to roam in the all-pervading light and love of God and Master."

If Rajarsi was so free even while he was here, how much more free is he now, when the heavy earthly vehicle has been cast aside! We shall miss his physical presence, but let us rejoice in his complete freedom and in the thought that he is wholly one with his Master in God.

In I Corinthians 15:58 we read: "Therefore, my beloved brethren, be ye steadfast, unmovable, always abounding in the work of the Lord."

By establishing Self-Realization Fellowship on a firm financial foundation and by the example of his ideal life, Rajarsi Janakananda indeed "abounded in the work of the Lord." Through his instrumentality many men will take heart and be lifted from darkness to light.

Bhagavad Gita XVIII:68 reads as follows: "He who, having shown the highest devotion to Me, shall declare this supreme secret among My devotees, shall come, beyond doubt, to Me." Rajarsi was one of those great souls to whom this verse refers. By daily meditation on God, he showed Him "the highest devotion"; and by his life and good works he "declared" or proved his deep desire to share with others the "supreme secret" of man's essential divinity.

The Gita continues: "Nor is there any among men who performeth dearer service to Me than he; nor is any other more beloved by Me." How inspiring is this divine assurance that God's heart is deeply touched by a beautiful life such as Rajarsi's!

May each of us not be engulfed in this dream-world of God's, which seems unsettling—even, at times, frightening. *Let us know the Divine Dreamer.* Like our beloved Rajarsi, let us make God the eternal Polestar of our lives.

RAJARSI JANAKANANDA AND REV. M. W. LEWIS

The president and the vice-president of SRF at the Hermitage, Encinitas, 1952. In a eulogy at Rajarsi's funeral, Dr. Lewis said: "By establishing Self-Realization Fellowship on a firm financial foundation and by the example of his ideal life, Rajarsi indeed 'abounded in the work of the Lord.' Through his instrumentality many men will take heart and be lifted from darkness to light."

The Eternal Friends

(Yoganandaji and St. Lynn)

BY PRABHAS CHANDRA GHOSH

Vice president, Yogoda Satsanga Society, Dakshineswar, India
(Written in 1937)

Paramahansaji journeyed far
Across vast lands and seas
To meet kindred spirits in the West.
The light of th' East was on his face,
A thousand mothers' love within his eyes,
All-conquering smiles upon his lips,
And in his words the ring of Realization.
On and on he moved in his quest.
As he spoke,
Truth threw off the masks of centuries
To reveal itself.
Quietly the other came,
A son of God—St. Lynn; seeking Silence
Amidst tumults of a dollar-driven age.
In tranquil communion they met.

Visions arose of the dim past
When, side by side, they had sat
On banks of the sacred Ganges,
In caves of hoary Himalayas,
To hear, within, the music of the spheres.
Oh, what meeting of two most ancient friends!
Not all the distance of Old World from the New
Nor all the vicissitudes of life
Had succeeded in keeping them apart.
Under the starry heavens, by babbling brooks,
In cliff-top hermitage 'bove Encinitas' splashing
    paradise seas,
In silence they met again and again.
Together they heard
And answered the call of th' Infinite.
Space melted; Time lost its wings;
And from the springs of united joy
Flowed a strong stream carrying waters of life
To countless souls struggling on rugged roads.
What else can these blessed travelers do
But sing His praise?
He who in divine mercy
Chose to bring His two sons
To preach His gospel together—
Love walking arm in arm with Faith,
Hope with Charity;
To dispel delusion-wraith
And perfume earth with wisdom, amity.

Mr. Lynn in a lettuce patch at Lynn Farms, Borrego Springs, California, New Year's Day, 1954. The 668-acre tract produced alfalfa, tomatoes, asparagus, grapes, and cantaloupes. Mr. Lynn was deeply interested in new methods for proper treatment of the soil.

The late president of Self-Realization Fellowship, who never drank or smoked, was a vegetarian for the last twenty-five years of his life. He ate cooked food only at dinner in the evenings. During the day he took fresh fruit juices and raw vegetable juices.

Press Comments About Mr. Lynn

The following appeared on the editorial page of the Kansas City Times, *Kansas City, Missouri, February 22, 1955.*

"The success story of James J. Lynn is a fabulous one that has been told and told again. Its beginning was in a tremendous natural ability and in a brilliancy for figures that removed a boy from a cotton farm and placed him on the high levels of big business. Its end found a man searching for something beyond financial success.

"That would seem entirely natural in considering the complex character of a man like James Lynn. He absorbed a belated education while working full time and was admitted to the bar at the age of 21. Three years later he was a certified public accountant. At 24 he was general manager of the U. S. Epperson Underwriting Company, and before he was 30 was the owner (along with a huge debt). Within a few years he had expanded into a half-dozen fields.

"His love of Nature and the fact that he reached a summit of material success at an early age must have contributed to his sincere interest of later years in religious mysticism. His death Sunday in California ends one of Kansas City's most remarkable stories of individual brilliance and achievement."

* * * * *

The following appeared in the Kansas City Star, *Kansas City, Missouri, February 27, 1955. The author is James S. Jackson, feature writer for the* Star.

"James J. Lynn was a very fine gentleman indeed—considerate, friendly, modest in demeanor....

"It was 'Jimmy' Lynn downtown, although few were closely acquainted with this unusual man. He was of youthful, alert appearance, springy of step and bareheaded, ruddy of complexion and with thinning hair; a man with a quick smile. He wore an open shirt, without necktie. That was the Jimmy Lynn Kansas City knew. Citizens were surprised to find that he of the springy step was already a highly successful businessman.

"Jimmy Lynn was one of the richer men in Kansas City. The fortune made through insurance underwriting was multiplied by lucky turns in the oil fields of Texas. He was easily the largest stockholder in the Union National Bank.

"Lynn's IQ Would Have Rung the Bell for Genius"

"He didn't appear to be a millionaire, but mentally he was lightning quick in perception and magic with figures. Mathematicswise, Lynn's IQ would have rung the bell for genius. We all know men who are marvels with figures, but no great shucks in business decisions. Lynn was also a man of sound business judgment. And he was extremely lucky. One needs a lucky touch to make millions in Texas oil from a Kansas City base....

"Before he was thirty, Jimmy Lynn headed the Epperson insurance underwriting concerns. It was not luck but the Lynn personality and capabilities that had attracted the attention of U. S. Epperson.

"Lynn himself said his success story was not one that could be duplicated today. Timing was a factor. Ahead of present-day tax laws he was able to buy a large, highly profitable business and to pay for it out of profits. But the deal had called for a sizable equity down-payment. A friend advanced the amount in cash.

A Huge Loan Secured Only by Lynn's Character

"The friend at the needful moment was the late E. F. Swinney of the First National Bank. The borrowing could not qualify as a bank loan. Swinney, watchful of a dollar though he was, advanced the money out of his own pocket. He, too, was paid out of earnings from the expanding business.

"Probably no other single incident in his career afforded Ed Swinney the satisfaction he got from his brief backing of Jimmy Lynn. Swinney, who held solvency to be a major virtue, often recounted that all payments from Lynn came ahead of schedule. He once remarked to this reporter that Lynn, the young man to whom he had lent helpful dollars, had passed him in wealth by two or three times. That was quite a few years ago, too. Swinney, incidentally, left an estate of three million dollars.

"Jimmy Lynn was an odd combination of the competent businessman and the philosopher who stressed closeness to universal forces. He felt he improved the quality of business letters by removing his shoes—inhibitors of foot respiration. The staff respected the keen mental alertness of the barefoot boss.

"Lynn assembled a large estate between Sixty-third Street and Meyer Boulevard. Here he developed in the late '20s a private nine-hole golf course. And there in the first hours of the young sun he brought himself close to Nature.

"Clad only in a loincloth, the astute businessman rolled through ex-

Rajarsi spent as much time as possible in the sunshine and fresh air. Here at the Encinitas hermitage in 1947 he performs a headstand with easy grace. A Kansas City reporter, describing Mr. Lynn's daily outdoor program, wrote:

"Clad only in a loincloth, the astute businessman rolled through exercises on the dewy lawn or lay prone for long periods to draw within himself forces from the good earth....He was happy for the ample privacy that attended the calisthenics. He could romp like a boy."

ercises on the dewy lawn, or lay prone for long periods to draw within himself forces from the good earth. These first hours of the day were important to Lynn, so he habitually had late hours for his office. Once at the office his quick perceptions soon had him abreast of the day.

"This daybreak rendezvous with the rising sun was something Lynn was quite ready to discuss. Of course, he was happy for the ample privacy that attended the calisthenics. He could romp like a boy....

Arranges Golf Course to Please His Older Friends

"Banker Swinney delighted in the short golf course. In fact, when the aging banker had to forego golf, the course was abandoned. Lynn sensed the pleasure his older friends took in their relatively low scores. In most standard golf courses every change introduces fresh hazards, but in the Lynn course every change eased existing difficulties.

"It had been Mr. Swinney's ambition to shoot a 75 on his seventy-fifth birthday, the occasion of a noteworthy party* on the Lynn estate in 1932. He did come in with a 76, quite happy and willing to over-look some concessions."

*The party was attended by about seventy-five guests, among them Judge Kenesaw Mountain Landis, the late commissioner of baseball; Mr. Mellville Taylor, at that time president of the First National Bank of Chicago; and the late Bishop Thomas F. Lillis.

Rajarsi in meditation, Encinitas, August 1953

Messages From Friends and SRF Centers

EMBASSY OF INDIA, WASHINGTON, D.C.: "Mr. G. L. Mehta, the Ambassador of India, regrets to learn the sad news of the death of Mr. James J. Lynn of the Self-Realization Fellowship, and wishes to convey his sincere condolences."

CONSULATE GENERAL OF INDIA, SAN FRANCISCO, CALIFORNIA. Mr. S. K. Banerji, Consul General of India, wrote: "I am grieved to hear that the president of the Fellowship, Rajarsi Janakananda, died. Though I did not have the opportunity of knowing him, I have heard a great deal about him, and would like to convey my condolences to the Fellowship."

DUCI DE KEREKJARTO, concert violinist: "The passing of our beloved Rajarsi is a great loss to all of us. Because he had God's love, he was a man of divine hope. He was at peace with himself and with others. I shall forever honor him for his reassuring voice: that of a good instructor, a faithful servant to the Master Yogananda."

SRF CENTER, MONTREAL, CANADA: "We are indeed sad that Rajarsi is no longer with us; but how wonderful that he is with Master!"

SRF CENTERS IN SWITZERLAND. Mrs. Helen Erba-Tissot wrote: "We must learn to say 'God alone,' and to meditate deeply enough to know what God through Master wishes from each of us. Rajarsi is surely with our beloved Master, and happy. We will go our way courageously, our minds firmly fixed on God."

MRS. G. J. WATUMULL, Watumull Foundation, Honolulu: "Although we did not know Mr. Lynn so well as we knew Paramahansa Yogananda, still we were very fond of Mr. Lynn and admired him tremendously. We all know that he has gone on to a larger and better life."

DR. WLADIMIR LINDENBERG, BERLIN, GERMANY. Dr. Lindenberg, director of a hospital for war-injured veterans in Berlin, wrote: "The news of our dear Rajarsi's *mahasamadhi* reached me today. After Paramahansaji's passing, Rajarsi was the father of Self-Realization Fellowship. I consider Rajarsi to have been a true representative of Paramahansaji, my beloved Guru. Now that Rajarsi is free from the bonds of the body, he will be able to wield a greater spiritual influence than ever before. God bless him, and you all, in the holy work. We will live in His joy, and love one another in the same joy."

SRF CENTER, LONDON, ENGLAND. Mrs. Gertrude White wrote: "It must have been Rajarsi's desire, if indeed he had one at all, to join Master. It is natural for us to miss the physical presence of loved ones; but what a wonderful thought it is that, if only we work with them, the great loving Masters will guide us also, as they have guided Rajarsi, from body-identification to soul-identification. Through the teachings of Paramahansaji, all our doubts have been removed. Our members had a long meditation on Thursday and Master seemed very close to us."

SRF CENTER, CALABAR, WEST AFRICA: "We held commemorative services on February 23rd and 25th. Lamenting Rajarsi's death, the whole center sends its heartfelt sympathy to Headquarters, praying that all be undiscouraged in carrying on the teachings of the Masters."

SRF MEDITATION GROUP, AUCKLAND, NEW ZEALAND. Mr. Reginald Howan wrote: "We who are so remotely placed in New Zealand have had little opportunity to know our late president and leader. In *Self-Realization Magazine,* however, we have observed his noble presence in pictures, and have read his inspired messages. The humble and unassuming manner in which he quietly took over the leadership on the passing of Paramahansa Yogananda spoke more than words to us of a remarkable personality. To follow immediately in the footsteps of such a Master was a great task for any man; the manner of Rajarsi's accomplishment endeared him to every discerning fellow-devotee on the path of Light.

"We salute Rajarsi Janakananda, who has joined the Great Ones beyond: Jesus, the Master of Galilee; Lahiri Mahasaya; Sri Yukteswar; the beloved Yogananda—that divine line of succession, of elder brethren. We are not separated from them, but rather are growing closer in our fuller realization of the Spirit whose love and power they manifested; a oneness that makes this Self-Realization Fellowship of ours a living power to do good, to destroy evil, and to assist mankind in re-establishing its rightful divine heritage."

(LEFT) Rajarsi Janakananda, Borrego Springs, California, 1954. (RIGHT) The bedroom in which Rajarsi's death occurred in his home at Lynn Farms, Borrego Springs. In the niche above are pictures of Christ (*center*), of Mahavatar Babaji and Lahiri Mahasaya (*top*), and of Sri Yukteswar and Paramahansa Yogananda (*bottom*).

Mr. Lynn said: "It is within the power of every one of us to attain true wisdom. We have to make the effort. It is up to us. We must meditate to attain deep faith. After we have received the first contact of God, we should then seek to develop the contact into greater and greater consciousness.

"Paramahansaji doesn't ask his students to accept anything as matter of belief only. 'Practice *Kriya Yoga,*' he says, 'and discover for yourself the glories of the soul within.'"

A Letter From Mexico City

BY YOGACHARYA J. M. CUARÓN

Leader of SRF Center in Mexico Until His Passing in 1967

In the past few years Rajarsi was extremely kind and considerate toward me. During the September week in 1951 that I spent in Encinitas, he and I used to meditate in Master's study every night from eight p.m. until midnight. Many times he told me: "Master is right here with us, and is very much pleased."

One night Rajarsi remarked that he did not have any personal desires, that the only desires he had were Master's desires. "As our Guru had wished to visit Mexico again," he said, "now I hope to be able to arrange to visit Mexico." Though that wish was not fulfilled, I am happy that Rajarsi harbored it.

Last year, too, when I visited Encinitas, Rajarsi called me three times to his apartment to meditate with him and to give me his blessings. On these occasions he would pat my hand and head in the same way that Master used to do, with the same gestures and expressions. I hardly knew whether it were Rajarsi or Master sitting before me.

On February 22, 1955, our members in Mexico City held a meeting dedicated to Rajarsi's memory. Our meditation was long and deep, and many of us felt his holy presence amongst us.

On March 8th we held commemorative services for the *mahasamadhis* of Paramahansaji and his guru Sri Yukteswarji. A brief talk on their sacred lives was followed by an hour of meditation. The meeting was solemn and beautiful. Each student brought flowers; the room was fragrant with the odors of flowers and incense. The attendance was large, and included two students from our Armenia SRF Center in the republic of Colombia in South America.

Before the meeting started I requested the students to leave the room quietly after the meditation was over, without speaking one to another, in order that all might carry with them the high spiritual vibrations of the meeting.

The meditation period ended with a playing of a recording of Master's voice, made at the dedication services on August 20, 1950, of the SRF Lake Shrine in Pacific Palisades. His closing words were: "Until we meet again. Peace, Om, Christ. I bow to you all."

Yogoda Math, YSS headquarters in Dakshineswar, India, held services for Rajarsi Janakananda on Feb. 23rd, the same date that funeral services for him were held in Los Angeles. The altar above displays pictures, lovingly garlanded, of Yoganandaji and Rajarsi.

Services at Yogoda Math, India, March 7th. Two photographs of Rajarsi *(bottom)* flank Paramahansaji's picture on memorial altar.

Services for Rajarsi in India

In 1917 Paramahansa Yogananda founded Yogoda Satsanga Society of India. In 1920 he established his international headquarters in America, translating the name in the West as Self-Realization Fellowship.

YOGODA MATH, DAKSHINESWAR, WEST BENGAL, YSS headquarters in India. On February 28th Sri Prabhas Chandra Ghosh, vice-president of the Society, sent to the Los Angeles international headquarters the following cable:

"India shares with the rest of the Self-Realization Fellowship world the deepest sorrow at the passing of our beloved president, Rajarsi Janakanandaji. We realize he has been called to the side of Master and that both, from above, will continue to guide us. Members here held memorial services for Rajarsiji on February 23rd to coincide with the time of his funeral in Los Angeles. All members observed a mourning period of fasting and prayer. On Sunday, February 27th, our members gathered again for a memorial service."

Yogoda Math sent a printed card to all YSS members in India, inviting them to attend, on March 7th in Dakshineswar, a joint memorial service for Rajarsiji and Paramahansa Yoganandaji. On that date a large gathering took part in the program of the all-day meeting. Readings from the Bhagavad Gita and the Bible started at eight a.m. and were followed by periods of meditation, prayer, and devotional chanting; by practice of *Hong-Sau* and *Kriya Yoga;* and by a period of Yogoda rejuvenation exercises as taught by Paramahansaji. From four to five p.m. the audience heard readings from Master's books—*Autobiography of a Yogi, Whispers from Eternity,* and *The Master Said.*

Letter From Yogoda Devotees

The following letter, dated February 27th, 1955, was sent to the head-quarters in Los Angeles from Yogoda Math, Dakshineswar, and signed by Prabhas Chandra Ghosh and a large representation of Yogoda members.

"The news of the death of our beloved leader, Rajarsi Janakananda, has given us a great shock. We had been looking forward eagerly to the day when we would be able to pay our respects to him here on the soil of India. It breaks our hearts to know that this, our dearest of wishes, must go unfulfilled.

"The Two Brothers, Bound by the Tie of Eternal Friendship"

"We can only submit to the will of the Divine Mother. We realize that Rajarsiji has joined Master and that the two brothers bound by the tie of eternal friendship will look after all of us.

"It was Master who taught us to love and adore Rajarsiji; his saintly life has long been before us as a great ideal. It will continue for all time to inspire travelers on the path of Self-realization.

Members attending the memorial service for Paramahansaji and Rajarsi at Yogoda Math, Dakshineswar, on March 7th, stand in silence during an intermission.

"We are greatly encouraged by the message of your continuing loving interest in the work started by Paramahansaji in this country. May we of SRF-YSS remain indissolubly united to spread the liberating message of our beloved Masters."

"His End Was Befitting the Great Yogi That He Was"

Shortly after Rajarsiji's passing, Sri Daya Mata sent to the Dakshineswar headquarters a letter of details about the beautiful manner in which he passed. In reply, Sri Prabhas Chandra Ghosh (who had met Rajarsiji in California in 1954) said: "His has been a wonderful life, and its end was befitting the great yogi that he was."

YOGODA BRAHMACHARYA VIDYALAYA, RANCHI, INDIA (residential high school for boys, founded by Paramahansa Yogananda in 1918). Brahmachari Animananda wrote: "On March 7th we observed with great devotion the commemoration of the *mahasamadhi* of our guru, Paramahansa Yogananda; and held a service sacred to the memory of our revered late president, Rajarsi Janakananda. The meeting lasted all day, from nine-thirty in the morning until nine at night. The numerous devotees present observed fasting until *prasad* (blessed food) was distributed at three o'clock. The services started with *puja* (divine worship) and ended with *kirtan* (religious chanting). There were readings from the *Vedas* and from *Yogi Kathamrita* (Bengali edition of *Autobiography of a Yogi*). Sri Ram Kishore Roy, who presided, gave a long address on the divine lives of Paramahansaji and Rajarsiji."

In a later letter, Brahmachari Animananda, secretary, YSS Ashram, Ranchi, wrote: "I am sorry I had no opportunity to sit at Rajarsiji's feet. His life, however, teaches me the lesson of selflessness and of wholly dedicating oneself to God and Guru. Our aim should be to adore the example set by him and thereby to please our Guru, who called Rajarsiji his 'blessed, beloved, little one.'"

SANANDA LAL GHOSH, CALCUTTA, INDIA. Sananda, younger brother of Paramahansa Yogananda, and leader of the YSS Center in Calcutta, wrote: "I have just heard the heartrending news of the death of Rajarsiji. I am sure he could not bear the separation from his Master and has joined him."

THE LINE OF MASTERS
BEHIND PARAMAHANSA YOGANANDA

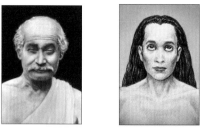 

Lahiri Mahasaya   Mahavatar Babaji   Sri Yukteswar

(An artist, with Paramahansaji's help, drew the picture of Babaji.)

Mahavatar Babaji

Mahavatar Babaji revived in this age the lost scientific meditation technique of *Kriya Yoga*. In bestowing *Kriya* initiation on his disciple Lahiri Mahasaya, Babaji said, "The *Kriya Yoga* that I am giving to the world through you in this nineteenth century is a revival of the same science that Krishna gave millenniums ago to Arjuna; and that was later known to Patanjali and Christ, and to St. John, St. Paul, and other disciples."

In 1920, Mahavatar Babaji came to Yoganandaji's home in Calcutta, where the young monk sat deeply praying for divine assurance about the mission he was soon to undertake. Babaji said to him: "Follow the behests of your guru [Sri Yukteswar] and go to America....You are the one I have chosen to spread the message of *Kriya Yoga* in the West. *Kriya Yoga,* the scientific technique of God-realization, will ultimately spread in all lands and aid in harmonizing the nations through man's personal, transcendental perception of the Infinite Father."

Lahiri Mahasaya (1828–1895), Disciple of Babaji

Lahiri Mahasaya was Babaji's chief 19th-century disciple. Though he was a man of family and business responsibilities, Lahiri Mahasaya's divine illumination attracted to him thousands of disciples in India.

Sri Yukteswar (1855–1936), Disciple of Lahiri Mahasaya

Sri Yukteswar was a disciple of Lahiri Mahasaya, and guru of Sri Yogananda. The beautiful lives of these three Masters are described in *Autobiography of a Yogi.*

Sri Yogananda (1893–1952), Disciple of Sri Yukteswar

Yogananda was the first great master of India to live in the West for a long period (over thirty years). He initiated 100,000 students in Yoga, the science of spiritual development. Through his books and his lessons for home study, and the establishment of monastic centers for training teachers, Paramahansa Yogananda ensured the continuance of the worldwide mission given to him by Mahavatar Babaji.

Yoganandaji a Premavatar, "Incarnation of Love"

Babaji is a *Mahavatar,* "Great Avatar (Divine Incarnation)"; Lahiri Mahasaya was a *Yogavatar,* "Incarnation of Yoga"; and Sri Yukteswar was a *Jnanavatar,* "Incarnation of Wisdom."

Rajarsi Janakananda bestowed on his guru, Paramahansa Yogananda, the title of *Premavatar,* "Incarnation of Love."

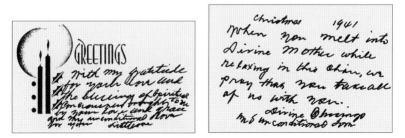

CHRISTMAS CARDS, SENT TO PARAMAHANSA YOGANANDA,
HANDWRITTEN BY RAJARSI JANAKANANDA

(LEFT) Rajarsi Janakananda has written: "With my gratitude for your love and the blessings of spiritual consciousness brought to me by your love and grace and by my unconditional love for you. *(signed)* LITTLE ONE" Master often called his disciple "Little One," because of Mr. Lynn's humility. Mr. Lynn signed himself as "Little One" in nearly all his letters to Master.

(RIGHT) Rajarsi has written: "Christmas, 1941. When you melt into Divine Mother while relaxing in this chair, we pray that you take all of us with you. Divine blessings and unconditional love."

This card was attached to a Christmas gift from Rajarsi: a reclining-type chair. From time to time Master would sit in the chair, enwrapped in the peace of *samadhi* (superconsciousness). The disciples around him were awefully aware that in his presence was a shower of blessings.

Paramahansa Yogananda

"The ideal of love for God and service to humanity found full expression in the life of Paramahansa Yogananda....Though the major part of his life was spent outside India, still he takes his place among our great saints. His work continues to grow and shine ever more brightly, drawing people everywhere on the path of the pilgrimage of the Spirit."

In these words, the Government of India paid tribute to the founder of Self-Realization Fellowship/Yogoda Satsanga Society of India, upon issuing a commemorative stamp in his honor on March 7, 1977, the twenty-fifth anniversary of his passing.

Paramahansa Yogananda began his life's work in India in 1917 with the founding of a "how-to-live" school for boys, where modern educational methods were combined with yoga training and instruction in spiritual ideals. In 1920 he was invited to Boston as India's representative to an International Congress of Religious Liberals. Subsequent lectures in Boston, New York, and Philadelphia were enthusiastically received, and in 1924 he embarked on a cross-continental speaking tour.

For the next decade Paramahansaji traveled extensively, giving lectures and classes in which he instructed thousands of men and women in the yoga science of meditation and balanced spiritual living. In 1925 he established the Self-Realization Fellowship International Headquarters in Los Angeles, and from there the spiritual and humanitarian work he began continues today under the guidance of one of his foremost disciples, Sri Daya Mata, president of Self-Realization Fellowship. In addition to publishing Paramahansa Yogananda's writings, lectures, and informal talks (including a comprehensive series of lessons on the science of *Kriya Yoga* meditation), the society oversees Self-Realization Fellowship temples, retreats, and meditation centers around the world; monastic training programs; and a Worldwide Prayer Circle, which serves as a channel to help bring healing to those in need and greater peace and harmony among all nations.

Quincy Howe, Jr., Ph.D., Professor of Ancient Languages, Scripps College, wrote: "Paramahansa Yogananda brought to the West not only India's perennial promise of God-realization, but also a practical method by which spiritual aspirants from all walks of life may progress rapidly toward that goal. Originally appreciated in the West only on the most lofty and abstract level, the spiritual legacy of India is now accessible as practice and experience to all who aspire to know God, not in the beyond, but in the here and now....Yogananda has placed within the reach of all the most exalted methods of contemplation."

The life and teachings of Paramahansa Yogananda are described in his *Autobiography of a Yogi* (see page 191).

AIMS AND IDEALS
OF
SELF-REALIZATION FELLOWSHIP

As set forth by Paramahansa Yogananda, Founder

Sri Daya Mata, President

To disseminate among the nations a knowledge of definite scientific techniques for attaining direct personal experience of God.

To teach that the purpose of life is the evolution, through self-effort, of man's limited mortal consciousness into God Consciousness; and to this end to establish Self-Realization Fellowship temples for God-communion throughout the world, and to encourage the establishment of individual temples of God in the homes and in the hearts of men.

To reveal the complete harmony and basic oneness of original Christianity as taught by Jesus Christ and original Yoga as taught by Bhagavan Krishna; and to show that these principles of truth are the common scientific foundation of all true religions.

To point out the one divine highway to which all paths of true religious beliefs eventually lead: the highway of daily, scientific, devotional meditation on God.

To liberate man from his threefold suffering: physical disease, mental inharmonies, and spiritual ignorance.

To encourage "plain living and high thinking"; and to spread a spirit of brotherhood among all peoples by teaching the eternal basis of their unity: kinship with God.

To demonstrate the superiority of mind over body, of soul over mind.

To overcome evil by good, sorrow by joy, cruelty by kindness, ignorance by wisdom.

To unite science and religion through realization of the unity of their underlying principles.

To advocate cultural and spiritual understanding between East and West, and the exchange of their finest distinctive features.

To serve mankind as one's larger Self.

Books by Paramahansa Yogananda

Available at bookstores or online at www.yogananda-srf.org

Autobiography of a Yogi

Autobiography of a Yogi *(Audiobook, read by Ben Kingsley)*

God Talks With Arjuna: The Bhagavad Gita
(A New Translation and Commentary)

The Second Coming of Christ: The Resurrection of the Christ Within You
(A revelatory commentary on the original teachings of Jesus)

The Collected Talks and Essays
Volume I: Man's Eternal Quest
Volume II: The Divine Romance
Volume III: Journey to Self-realization

Wine of the Mystic: The Rubaiyat of Omar
Khayyam—A Spiritual Interpretation

The Science of Religion

Whispers from Eternity

Songs of the Soul

Sayings of Paramahansa Yogananda

Scientific Healing Affirmations

Where There Is Light: Insight and Inspiration
for Meeting Life's Challenges

In the Sanctuary of the Soul: A Guide to Effective Prayer

Inner Peace: How to Be Calmly Active and Actively Calm

How You Can Talk With God

Metaphysical Meditations

The Law of Success

Cosmic Chants

*A complete catalog of books and audio/video recordings—including rare archival
recordings of Paramahansa Yogananda—is available on request or online at
www.yogananda-srf.org*

Self-Realization Fellowship Lessons

The scientific techniques of meditation taught by Paramahansa Yogananda,
including *Kriya Yoga,* are presented in the *Self-Realization Fellowship Lessons.*
For further information, please ask for the free introductory booklet *Undreamed-
of Possibilities.*

SELF-REALIZATION FELLOWSHIP
3880 San Rafael Avenue • Los Angeles, CA 90065-3298
TEL (323) 225-2471 • FAX (323) 225-5088
www.yogananda-srf.org

Also published by Self-Realization Fellowship...

AUTOBIOGRAPHY OF A YOGI

This acclaimed autobiography presents a fascinating portrait of one of the preeminent spiritual figures of our time. With engaging candor, eloquence, and wit, Paramahansa Yogananda narrates the inspiring chronicle of his life—the experiences of his remarkable childhood, encounters with many saints and sages during his youthful search throughout India for an illumined teacher, ten years of training in the hermitage of a revered yoga master, and the thirty years that he lived and taught in America. Also recorded here are his meetings with Mahatma Gandhi, Rabindranath Tagore, Luther Burbank, the Catholic stigmatist Therese Neumann, and other celebrated spiritual personalities of East and West.

Autobiography of a Yogi is at once a beautifully written account of an exceptional life and a profound introduction to the ancient science of Yoga and its time-honored tradition of meditation. The author clearly explains the subtle but definite laws behind both the ordinary events of everyday life and the extraordinary events commonly termed miracles. His absorbing life story thus becomes the background for a penetrating and unforgettable look at the ultimate mysteries of human existence.

First published in 1946 and enlarged by Paramahansa Yogananda in 1951, the book has been kept in print continuously by Self-Realization Fellowship. It has been translated into eighteen languages and is widely used as a text and reference work in colleges and universities. Considered a modern spiritual classic, *Autobiography of a Yogi* has found its way into the hearts of millions of readers around the world.

"A rare account." —*The New York Times*

"A fascinating and clearly annotated study." —*Newsweek*

"There has been nothing before, written in English or in any other European language, like this presentation of Yoga." —*Columbia University Press*

"Sheer revelation...should help the human race to understand itself better... autobiography at its very best...told with delightful wit and compelling sincerity...as fascinating as any novel." —*News-Sentinel, Fort Wayne, Indiana*

"These pages reveal, with incomparable strength and clarity...a personality of such unheard-of greatness that from beginning to end, the reader is left breathless....We must credit this important biography with the power to bring about a spiritual revolution." —*Schleswig-Holsteinische Tagespost, Germany*